Second Edition
Skillful 2

Listening & Speaking Student's Book

Authors: David Bohlke and Robyn Brinks Lockwood
Series Consultant: Dorothy E. Zemach

Grammar	Speaking	Study skills	Unit outcomes
Use discourse markers for adding reasons or details	Notice and practice weak forms Practice giving reasons and explanations Analyze and evaluate which charity to donate to	Managing work and study	Listen for examples to understand evidence in arguments Listen for details in a lecture to follow its organization Discuss, compare, and evaluate two charities
Use relative clauses to add further information	Notice and practice consonant clusters Offer advice and suggestions Present ways to reduce food waste in your local town	Optimal learning to suit you	Practice listening for important information Listen to predict the content of a lecture Evaluate and present suggestions to reduce food waste
Use modal verbs for advice	Chunking a presentation Turn-taking Present a business plan to turn a failing business around	Getting the most out of discussion	Listen to understand a speaker's reasons Distinguish between similar sounds Work with a group to present a business plan
Use the simple past to order historical events	Notice and practice stress patterns in phrases connected with *and* Ask for clarification and repetition Present a timeline of your city	Time management	Listen for dates to understand a timeline Listen for time signals to understand when events happened Describe a timeline of a city's development
Use quantifiers to express approximate quantity	Notice and practice stress in modifiers before data Use discourse markers to compare and contrast Brainstorm, prepare, and present a small talk about passing exams	Studying for tests	Listen to understand key vocabulary in context Listen to summarize what you have heard Compare and contrast data in a presentation about exams

Grammar	Speaking	Study skills	Unit outcomes
Use modals in conditional sentences to give advice	Notice and practice consonant sounds at word boundaries Use different techniques to explain something you don't know the word for Brainstorm and discuss ways to reduce academic pressure	Enabling good discussion	Listen to understand how to support an argument Listen to understand cause and effect Analyze, evaluate, and give advice on how to minimize academic pressure
Use the present perfect tense with adverbs to talk about experiences	Notice and practice pausing and pacing speech Use key language to manage questions from the floor Brainstorm, prepare, and present a small talk about a problem you have had to solve	Increasing confidence when speaking	Listen to understand how a speech is organized Listen to identify problems and solutions Deliver a talk on a problem you have had to solve
Use the past progressive to tell a story or experience	Identify, distinguish, and pronounce words beginning with /g/ and /k/ Use words to express your attitude towards something Prepare and tell a factual or fictional story you know	Finding your creative streak	Listen to understand the order of events Listen to select key information to add to a diagram Tell a story
Use modal passives to describe processes and actions	Notice and practice stress with word suffixes Use different techniques to interact with a presenter Present a poster on the environment	Preparing a poster	Listen to identify pros and cons of an argument Listen to understand when and how to interact with a presenter Plan and deliver a poster presentation on the environment
Use indirect questions to be polite	Notice and practice citation, contrastive, and emphatic stress Use different techniques to refute an argument Hold a debate on the impact technology has on patient care	Argument: persuasion through reasons	Listen to understand how an argument is supported Listen to identify the speaker's attitude towards something Prepare for and participate in a debate on technology in medicine

To the student

Academic success requires so much more than memorizing facts. It takes skills. This means that a successful student can both learn and think critically.

Skillful gives you:

- Skills you need to succeed when reading and listening to academic texts
- Skills you need to succeed when writing for and speaking to different audiences
- Skills for critically examining the issues presented by a speaker or a writer
- Study skills for learning and remembering the English language and important information.

To successfully use this book, use these strategies:

Come to class prepared to learn. This means that you should show up well fed, well rested, and prepared with the proper materials. Watch the video online and look at the discussion point before starting each new unit.

Ask questions and interact. Learning a language is not passive. You need to actively participate. Help your classmates, and let them help you. It is easier to learn a language with other people.

Practice! Memorize and use new language. Use the *Skillful* online practice to develop the skills presented in the Student's Book. Review vocabulary on the review page.

Review your work. Look over the skills, grammar, and vocabulary from previous units. Study a little bit each day, not just before tests.

Be an independent learner, too. Look for opportunities to study and practice English outside of class, such as reading for pleasure and using the Internet in English. Remember that learning skills, like learning a language, takes time and practice. Be patient with yourself, but do not forget to set goals. Check your progress and be proud of your success! I hope you enjoy using *Skillful*!

Dorothy E. Zemach – Series Consultant

Opening page

Each unit starts with two opening pages. These pages get you ready to study the topic of the unit. There is a video to watch and activities to do before you start your class.

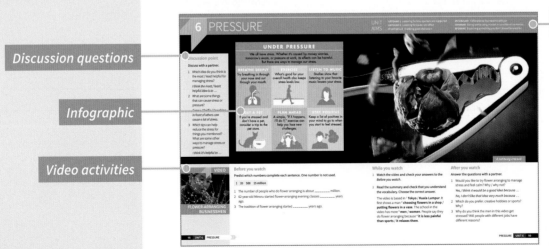

Unit aims

Discussion questions

Infographic

Video activities

Listening lessons

In every unit, there are two listening lessons and they present two different aspects of the unit topic and help you with ideas and language for your speaking task.

Vocabulary to prepare you for the listening activities.

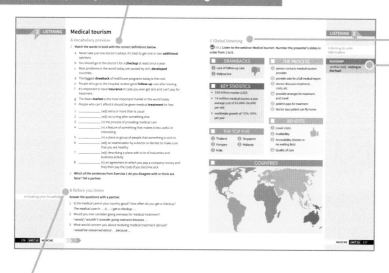

Every listening section helps you use a new listening skill.

Glossaries help you understand higher level words from the listening text.

Develop your listening skills in each part of the listening lesson.

Speaking lessons

After your listening lessons, there is a page for you to analyze a model answer to a speaking task. This will help you organize your ideas and language and prepare for your final task at the end of the unit.

First, analyze the model answer.

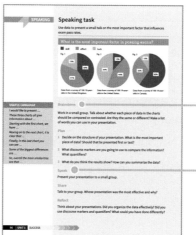

Brainstorm your speaking task and organize your ideas and language from the unit.

Finally, perform your speaking task.

Next, discuss your ideas.

1 SOCIETY

Discussion point

Discuss with a partner.

1 A lot of young people in the U.S. care about people receiving a good education. Do you think this is important?

2 What charities do people support where you live?

3 What type of charities do you think people should support?

WHAT DO YOU GIVE?

7 in 10 young adults in the U.S.A. support charitable causes

They do this by:

 Donating time

 Donating money

 Going to meetings and staying informed

 Sharing news and information online

Causes they care most about:

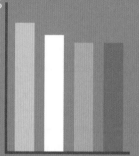

100%

88% care about receiving **good education**

80% care about finding new ways to **treat illnesses**

75% care about ways to save energy to **help the environment**

75% care about universal access to **healthcare**

VIDEO

A ROYAL VISIT

Before you watch

Read the statements and choose *T* (True) or *F* (False).

1 Charities only give money to people in need, nothing else.   T / F

2 There are hundreds of charities in almost every country around the world.   T / F

3 It's common for members of the British Royal Family to support charities.   T / F

4 Only women in the British Royal Family do charity work.   T / F

UNIT AIMS

LISTENING 1 Listening for examples
LISTENING 2 Listening for details
STUDY SKILL Managing work and study

VOCABULARY Verb and noun collocations
GRAMMAR Discourse markers for adding reasons or details
SPEAKING Giving reasons and explanations

Charity workers deliver supplies in Niger.

While you watch

Answer the questions.

1 What kind of charities does the Duchess of Cambridge work with?

2 What do **volunteers** do?

3 Why are the Duke and Duchess visiting the Child Bereavement UK charity?

4 How many charities do the Duke and Duchess of Cambridge visit in the video?

After you watch

Answer the questions with a partner.

1 The video says William and Kate "do their bit for society" by supporting various charities. Would you like to support a charity? Why / why not?

Yes, I'd like to because …

No, not really because …

2 How many charities do you think exist in your local community, and in your country? Explain what some of these charities do.

Community service

A Vocabulary preview

1 Circle the word or phrase that has a similar meaning to the words in bold.

1	**community service** (n)	a job	b education	c volunteering
2	**concept** (n)	a view	b opinion	c idea
3	**consider** (v)	a think about	b talk about	c worry about
4	**donate** (v)	a give	b receive	c change
5	**duty** (n)	a choice	b preference	c obligation
6	**fortunate** (adj)	a lucky	b unlucky	c unhappy
7	**institution** (n)	a charity	b organization	c individual
8	**recommendations** (n)	a tasks	b suggestions	c rules

2 Complete the sentences with the correct form of the words in bold from Exercise 1.

1 I am _____ enough to have my own car.

2 The university is the oldest educational _____ in this city.

3 I always _____ my old clothes to charity shops.

4 My school requires us to do _____. I visit sick people at the local hospital.

5 It's your_____ to take care of your parents when they are old.

6 My mother asked me to _____ volunteering my time to help others.

7 Can you explain the _____ of being prosocial to me?

8 I asked my college advisor for his _____ of the best medical schools.

B Before you listen

Preparing to listen

1 What do you consider to be community service? Check (✓) the following.

☐ building a house

☐ cleaning your room

☐ cooking dinner for your family

☐ helping your brother / sister with homework

☐ planting trees in the park

☐ reading to the blind

☐ teaching children

☐ visiting hospital patients

GLOSSARY

blind (n) unable to see

2 Work with a partner. Look at the list of community service projects from Exercise 1. Have you done any of these? Can you think of any other ideas?

C Global listening

🎧 **1.1** Listen to *Community service* and check (✓) the three main

☐ Community service includes volunteering time and service to h

☐ Volunteers usually serve people who have enough money or a good health.

☐ Volunteers work in different types of public institutions.

☐ Doing your duty is a form of community service.

☐ Caring about others has nothing to do with the person helping people receiving the help.

Peer check
↓
Build Confidence
↓
Get them talking.

1) *Starter* →
2) *Get them thinking*
2) *Language task*
3) *Review.*

Listening for examples

D Close listening

Speakers often give examples to support their ideas or arguments. There are phrases you can listen for to help you recognize when to expect an example:

For example …   *… like …*   *… such as …*

For instance …   *To illustrate, …*

A good way to note down examples is to write *e.g.*

community service   *e.g., tutoring, building houses*

1 🎧 **1.1** Listen to *Community service* again. Write one or two examples of each concept.

Community service   e.g., *volunteering*
Community institutions   e.g., _____
Work at hospitals   e.g., _____
Types of manual work   e.g., _____

2 🎧 **1.2** Listen to excerpts from *Community service*. Complete the sentences with the signal word or phrase used to give each example.

1 _____, some volunteers tutor children who need help in their studies in summer school programs.

2 A lot of volunteers work in hospitals. _____, they donate time to visiting patients who have no relatives or help busy doctors and nurses.

3 Sometimes volunteers do manual work _____ helping build a house or planting trees in a local park.

4 It could also be something very simple, _____ giving a ride to people who can't drive.

E Critical thinking

Discuss the questions.

1 Which things in the box are benefits and which are drawbacks of doing community service?

college applications   feel good   learning new skills
not enough money   not enough time   other duties   teamwork

2 How can doing community service help you achieve your future goals?

I think doing community service will help me by …

Study skills | Managing work and study

If you want to combine study and employment, it is worth investigating potential obstacles and ways of managing these.

If you are already in employment and have a good relationship with your employer, talk to them about how to manage work alongside study:

Could your study be used as professional development?

Can you do useful work-based projects that could be part of your degree?

Would your employer be willing to provide study leave, quiet space, and time to study at work, or support your costs?

Some jobs do not work well as work-study combinations, but other projects may still be possible.

© Stella Cottrell (2013)

1 Discuss these questions with a partner.

1 What kinds of charity work would you recommend for someone who wants to be a …

a doctor? _____

b teacher? _____

c gardener? _____

d psychologist? _____

2 What charity work would support what you are studying?

3 How can you balance charity work and study?

2 Rank these benefits to combining work and study from 1 (most useful) to 5 (least useful). Compare with a partner.

___ A wider range of experience and skills

___ Greater confidence in adult work settings

___ Increased responsibility

___ Professional and/or business awareness

___ Salary (how much work pays you)

3 Answer these questions with a partner.

1 What other benefits would combining work and study bring for you?

2 What arrangements would you need to make?

3 What kind of job combines well with the subject(s) you study?

Can money buy happiness?

A Vocabulary preview

1 Match the words in bold with the correct definitions.

1	**cause** (n)	a	a person you work with
2	**charity** (n)	b	cost a lot of money
3	**colleague** (n)	c	a test to find out what happens
4	**expensive** (adj)	d	an organization that supports people in need
5	**experiment** (n)	e	completely different from something else
6	**opposite** (adj)	f	existing at the beginning of a period or process
7	**original** (adj)	g	an organization that you support or work for
8	**provide** (v)	h	to give someone something they need

2 Complete the sentences with the correct word from Exercise 1.

1 The _____ the psychologist conducted determined that money can buy happiness.

2 Some people think it's a good idea to support a _____ by donating money or time.

3 José wants to buy a new car, but cars are very _____. He will need to save some money.

4 My _____ plan was to study on Friday, but when my friends called about dinner, I changed my plan and decided to study on Saturday instead.

5 Giving money to people that need it can _____ food or a bed for a night.

6 I often help my _____ when he has too much work to do.

7 I thought a lot of people volunteered, but actually the _____ is true.

8 Save the Children is a very big _____.

3 Discuss these questions with a partner.

1 Have you ever given money to a charity or worked with a charity? Did you enjoy it? Why / why not?

2 Which causes do you think are most important? Why?

3 What is the most expensive thing you have ever bought for yourself? For someone else?

B Before you listen

1 Discuss these questions with a partner.

1 When you have a little extra money, what do you spend it on?

2 When do you buy things for other people? Give an example of something you bought for someone else.

I like to buy …

I bought … for … because …

3 Do you think money can buy happiness? Why / why not?

2 You are going to hear a lecture on a psychology experiment. Number the points in the order you think you will hear them.

Predicting

___ Answer the question about the experiment

___ Ask a question about the experiment

___ Describe the experiment

___ Describe the results

C Global listening

 **1.3** Listen to *Can money buy happiness?* and complete these sentences about the main ideas with no more than two words.

Listening for the main ideas

1 The lecture is about _____ and _____.

2 First, the speaker experimented on a group of _____.

3 *Prosocial* means to use money to _____.

4 Helping others rather than helping themselves made these people _____.

5 Doing _____ things can make you just as happy as doing the _____ things.

6 The experiment was also done in a sales _____ in New Zealand.

GLOSSARY

piñata (n) a container filled with candy or presents that you hang from the ceiling at a party for children to hit with sticks and break

Listening for details

D Close listening

Detailed information is the facts and further information a speaker provides to support their main idea, such as numbers, places, examples, or evidence. Below are some phrases often used to indicate more detail will follow:

According to Dr. Smith, …   *Specifically, …*

Furthermore, it is believed that …

When you listen to something for the first time, it's a good idea to listen just to understand the topic and the speaker's opinion or aim. When you listen a second time, you can take notes on the detailed information you hear.

1 🔒 1.3 Listen to *Can money buy happiness?* again. Take notes on the two experiments. Use the exercise in *C Global listening* to help.

> *Question professor wants to answer*
>
> *Describe experiment*
>
> *Describe results*
>
> *Answer the question*

2 Work with a partner. Compare your notes from Exercise 1. Did they write down any details that you can add to your notes?

E Critical thinking

Discuss these questions in a group.

1 Do you believe money can buy happiness for people? Why / why not?

   I believe money can buy happiness because …
   I don't believe money can buy happiness because …

2 How did the listening text make you feel about giving money to others? Do you agree that this makes people happier?

Pronunciation for listening

Elision of vowel sounds

In words that have three or more syllables, speakers often miss out a vowel sound in order to say the word more easily and more quickly.

chocolate = choclate   interesting = intresting
camera = camra   beverage = bevrage
family = famly   evening = evning
vegetable = vegtable   history = histry

1 🎧 1.4 Listen to the words. Underline the letters you don't hear.

1 every
2 comparable
3 generally
4 different
5 favorite
6 reasonable
7 suppose
8 miserable

2 Read these sentences to a partner. Practice leaving out the vowel sounds.

1 I go to school every week.
2 The prices at the two stores are comparable.
3 My mother generally cooks a family dinner on Sunday.
4 My friends all have different majors.
5 My favorite subject is _____.
6 Be reasonable when planning time to work and study.
7 I suppose it is a good idea to do community service.
8 _____ is one thing that makes me miserable!

Vocabulary development

Verb and noun collocations

Collocations are words that are often used together. Collocations can be formed from different parts of speech. The most common type of collocation is verb and noun collocations. For example:

verb	+	noun
care for	+	others
do	+	community service
donate	+	money or clothing or time
give	+	time or money
make	+	a difference
take	+	a break or a call

1 Match the verbs in the box with the correct nouns to make common collocations.

| answer do give make manage order pay take |

1 _____ homework

2 _____ a presentation

3 _____ the bed

4 _____ the phone

5 _____ your workload

6 _____ a drink

7 _____ a chance

8 _____ attention

2 Answer the questions with a partner.

1 When did you last take a break?

2 What is one thing you think will make a difference to someone's happiness?

3 When did you last donate time to something or someone?

4 What is one good way to care for others?

5 Do you know anyone who does community service? Who?

6 When was the last time someone gave you their time? What was it for?

Academic words

1 Choose the best definitions for the words in bold.

1 You can take an **intermediate** English test if you already know some of the language.

2 Lucinda didn't like anything to interrupt her **normal** work-study hours.

3 The **principal** aim of community service is to help those less fortunate.

4 Being prosocial is an **abstract** idea.

5 Pamela read the instructions on the **label** of her food to see how to cook it.

6 Jacques is **cooperative**; he always helps new volunteers when they first start community service.

7 Liza will make a **revision** to her college application after she completes her community service.

8 Community service at the hospital **benefits** the patients, doctors, and volunteers.

a _____ (adj) exist as thoughts but are not physical things that you can touch

b _____ (adj) main or most important

c _____ (v) helps

d _____ (n) a change or improvement to something

e _____ (adj) willing to do what you ask

f _____ (n) piece of paper or material that gives information or instructions about something

g _____ (adj) expected; not unusual or surprising

h _____ (adj) a level between beginning and advanced

2 Work with a partner. Answer the questions and explain your answers.

1 Do you think community service can benefit your college application?

2 What is one abstract idea you can think of?

3 Talk about what a normal Friday is like for you.

4 Why is it helpful to have labels on food or medicine?

5 What have you recently made a revision to? How did you change it?

6 Talk about someone you know who is cooperative. What makes them cooperative?

7 What do you think is the principal part of a college application?

8 What could you do to move from intermediate level in English to advanced?

Speaking model

You will learn how to give examples, provide reasons and add information, and to pronounce verbs that end in –*ed* or –*ing*. You are then going to present reasons to support a charity of your choice.

A Analyze

Work in a small group. Read the model and match the beginning of the statements with reasons or details.

1 It helps provide money and support
2 I think Doctors Without Borders deserves our money because
3 In addition to providing help to those affected by diseases or natural disasters,

a to enable children to do things they can't normally do.
b it also helps people who are victims in parts of the world that are suffering from conflict.
c it gives emergency medical help to people all over the world.

Yoohee: What kind of charity should we contribute our money to?

Carolina: There are a lot to choose from. We could choose a charity that is dedicated to health because I think it's really important. Make-A-Wish and Doctors Without Borders are both big charities that do lots of good work.

Yoohee: Those sound interesting. What do they do?

Carolina: Make-A-Wish is a charity that aims to make sick children's wishes come true. It helps provide money and support to enable children to do things they can't normally do. Doctors Without Borders is a charity that helps people in countries affected by war.

Yoohee: Wow. They both sound impressive. Which would you like to donate to?

Carolina: I think Doctors Without Borders deserves our money because it gives emergency medical help to people all over the world. In addition to providing help to those affected by diseases or natural disasters, it also helps people who are victims in parts of the world that are suffering from conflict.

Yoohee: How does Doctors Without Borders spend its donation money?

Carolina: Well, over 88% of their donation money is spent on the people it supports. Only 1% is spent on management, resulting in most of the money going to helping people!

Yoohee: Most of the money actually goes to the people. That makes the decision easy, I think. I agree that this is the best charity to donate to.

B Discuss

1 What reason finally convinces Yoohee to agree to Carolina's choice of charity?
2 How does Carolina explain her reasons for her choice?

Grammar

Discourse markers for adding reasons or details

Discourse markers are words or phrases that let the listener know what the speaker is trying to say. They help the speaker connect ideas to make the purpose of statements clear.

Below are some of the most common discourse markers we use for adding reasons or details:

Also, …

In addition, / Additionally, …

Another (reason is) …

Plus, …

Furthermore, …

What's more, …

Besides, …

In writing, these discourse markers are often followed by a comma (,), which allows the speaker time to consider what they are going to say.

1   Connect the two sentences using a discourse marker.

   1   You can volunteer at the hospital because they need people to visit patients. They need people to help the nurses.

   2   Jana worked for 16 hours without a break and she needs to sleep. She doesn't want to get sick.

   3   Peter might do work experience at the hospital because he wants to go to medical school. He wants to help sick people.

   4   Lily should become president of the volunteer group because she volunteers the most hours. She knows a lot of charities.

   5   Kenichi donated all his clothes to the less fortunate. He donated some money to the food bank in his local community.

2   Read the situations. Write a new sentence adding another reason.

   1   Cassie applied for a job as a teacher because she likes working with children.

   _____.

   2   Eduardo wants to volunteer his time. He could read to the blind.

   _____.

   3   Mei-li wants to donate some money to charity. She could give some of it to charities supporting international aid.

   _____.

   4   Tay hopes to study in the United States next summer. He would like to use the opportunity to improve his English.

   _____.

3   Compare your answers from Exercise 2 with a partner.

Speaking skill

There are several discourse markers we use to let listeners know we are giving a reason or explanation for something. These usually either focus on the cause or the effect of something.

Cause	Effect
… may be due to …	*resulting in …*
… may be because …	*hence, …*
one consequence of …	*one effect of … is …*

*The reason I know a lot about this charity **may be due to** my brother working with them for a year when he finished medical school.*

*Only 1% is spent on management, **resulting in** most of the money going to helping people!*

1 Choose one of the phrases in the *Giving reasons and explanations* box to complete the sentences.

1 The charity is able to help a lot of people, which _____ many people care about helping others.

2 The charity is very successful _____ lots of people donating money on a regular basis, _____ it being able to help a lot of people.

3 _____ charity work is that more people are supported all over the world.

4 The charity's success _____ excellent teamwork.

2 Work with a partner. Explain why the following statement might or might not be true.

> *Small charities often give more money to the people they help than large charities.*

Pronunciation for speaking

Weak forms

Function words, the words that don't tell us what the sentence is about, such as *and*, *a, can, the, on*, *by,* and *to,* are usually pronounced in their weak form. These words do not carry the main content, so they are not stressed. Weak forms like these usually have the schwa (ə) sound as its vowel sound.

Content words, such as nouns, verbs, adjectives, and adverbs, carry the meaning of the sentence. They are usually pronounced in their strong form.

1   🎧 1.5 Listen and select the number of words in each sentence.

1   5   6   7
2   6   7   8
3   9   10   11
4   7   8   9
5   6   7   8
6   6   7   8

2   Underline the weak forms in these sentences.

1   I went to the market today to buy apples.
2   Daniel wrote an essay about volunteering in his home country.
3   Julie and Nadia are in the same class.
4   My teacher said that I have to study for my test.

3   Practice saying the sentences from Exercise 2 with a partner. Did you notice the difference between the strong and weak forms?

Speaking task

Analyze and evaluate which charity to donate to.

Brainstorm

Your teacher will divide you into Group A and B. Your group will prepare a charity profile for one of two charities. Turn to page 188. Group A reads about *Helping the World to Read*. Group B reads about *Rebuilding Helper*.

Make a list of reasons why your charity should receive funding.

Plan

Rank your list of reasons. Put the reason your group feels most strongly about first.

Speak

Present the ideas on your list to one of the other groups. Remember to add reasons and explanations. At the end, ask whether they would donate to the charity you chose based on your argument.

I think we should donate here because …
Another reason we should donate to this organization is …

Share

Work with a third group. Talk about your first discussion and the response you got. What could you have done to make your argument more persuasive?

Reflect

Look back at the ideas presented in the unit and answer the question "What makes the best kind of charity?" with a partner.

Review

Wordlist

MACMILLAN DICTIONARY

Vocabulary preview

cause (n) ***	donate (v) *	opposite (adj) ***
charity (n) ***	duty (n) ***	original (adj) ***
colleague (n) ***	expensive (adj) ***	provide (v) ***
community service (n)	experiment (n) ***	recommendation (n) **
concept (n) ***	fortunate (adj) **	
consider (v) ***	institution (n) ***	

Vocabulary development

care for others (phrase)	donate money/clothing/time (phrase)	make a difference (phrase)
do community service (phrase)	give time/money (phrase)	take a break/call (phrase)

Academic words

abstract (adj) **	intermediate (adj) **	principal (adj) ***
benefit (v) ***	label (n) **	revision (n) **
cooperative (adj) *	normal (adj) ***	

Academic words review

Complete the sentences using the words in the box.

benefit   intermediate   normal   principal   revision

1 I had to make one _____ to my essay because it was incorrect.
2 The _____ idea behind Tom's essay is to demonstrate that scientists can predict earthquakes.
3 Around 30 degrees is the _____ temperature in summer.
4 You will _____ from learning and practicing good study skills.
5 Mariam speaks English well. She is an _____ student.

Unit review

Listening 1	☐	I can listen for examples.
Listening 2	☐	I can listen for details.
Study skill	☐	I can manage my work and study commitments.
Vocabulary	☐	I can use a range of collocations of verbs with nouns.
Grammar	☐	I can use expressions to add reasons or details.
Speaking	☐	I can use expressions to give reasons and explanations.

Discussion point

Discuss with a partner.

1 Which food group in the infographic do you eat the most of? Which do you eat the least of?

2 Which do you waste the most? Why?

3 Why do you think people, restaurants, and supermarkets waste food?

4 What do you think governments and individuals can do to reduce food waste?

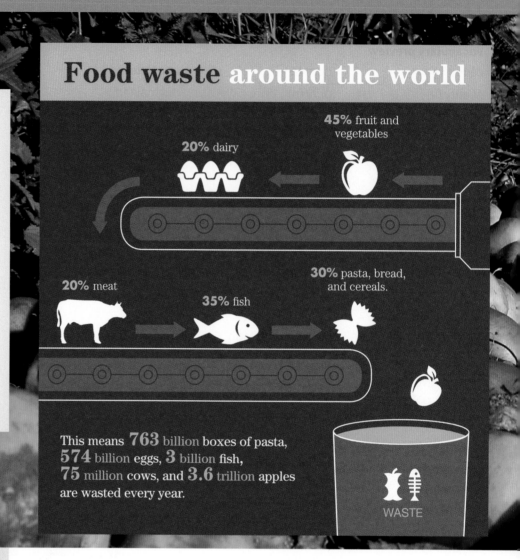

Food waste around the world

20% dairy

45% fruit and vegetables

20% meat

35% fish

30% pasta, bread, and cereals.

This means **763** billion boxes of pasta, **574** billion eggs, **3** billion fish, **75** million cows, and **3.6** trillion apples are wasted every year.

WASTE

VIDEO

SHELF LIFE

Before you watch

1 Work with a partner and discuss the meaning of the words and phrases in bold.

1 Why is food **wasted**?

2 Would you eat food that is **out of date**? Why / why not?

3 Which of types of food go **moldy,** and which go hard and **stale** if they are out of date? (e.g., fruit, cookies, bread, cake, cheese)

4 Why does food **go bad**?

5 When you were little, did your parents make you eat all your food? Or did you **throw away** food that you didn't eat?

2 Take turns asking and answering the questions with your partner.

UNIT AIMS

LISTENING 1 Listening for emphasis of main ideas
LISTENING 2 Predicting
STUDY SKILL Optimal learning

VOCABULARY Phrasal verbs
GRAMMAR Relative clauses
SPEAKING Offering advice and suggestions

Spoiled apples.

3   Work with a partner. Predict which of these you will see or hear in the video and discuss why they will appear.

An apple might be used in an experiment to see if it goes moldy.

apples	bottles
bread	crab shells
test tube	grapefruit
petri dish	group of young students
plastic	mold
drink can	white mice

While you watch

Watch the video and check your answers.

After you watch

Answer the questions with a partner.

1   Why is normal plastic bad for storing bread?

2   Why is the new plastic better for food and for your health?

3   Should governments spend money researching new types of food packaging? Why / why not?

Food waste

A Vocabulary preview

1 Match the words in bold with the correct definitions.

1	**agriculture** (n)	a	something that requires a lot of skill or effort to achieve
2	**billion** (n)	b	the material left after use
3	**challenge** (n)	c	the lack of food that can cause illness or death
4	**feed** (v)	d	the number 1,000,000,000
5	**hunger** (n)	e	to give food to someone or something
6	**profit** (n)	f	how to solve a problem or deal with a bad situation
7	**solution** (n)	g	the study of farming
8	**waste** (n)	h	the money made by selling something

2 Complete the sentences with the correct word from Exercise 1.

1 The United States still faces a big _____ because 5–10% of the population does not have enough food.

2 One way supermarkets can help solve the _____ problem is to donate out-of-date food to charities to make sure people have enough to eat.

3 There are many charities that use donations to _____ people who don't have enough to eat.

4 The professor explained that food _____ can be used to feed animals or help land to grow.

5 Mikhail is studying _____ because he plans to manage his family's farm when he graduates.

6 Over a _____ tons of food is wasted every year, contributing to both environmental and hunger problems around the world.

7 Grocery stores don't want to lose _____ by throwing away fruit and vegetables that are not sold.

8 The university has not yet thought of a _____ for all the food wasted in the school's cafeterias.

B Before you listen

Activating prior knowledge

Answer these questions with a partner.

1 Have you ever thrown food out? Why did you throw the food out?

2 What problems do you think wasting food can cause?

3 How could people try to solve those problems?

C Global listening

It's good to be able to recognize which ideas are being emphasized when you are listening because it helps you understand and remember important information.

There are several techniques we use to introduce emphasis.

- Focus on the way a speaker highlights or signals that important information is coming next.

  We are going to discuss … It is important to note …

- Listen for phrases that indicate when the speaker is going to summarize a point.

  In other words, … Basically, …

- Listen for words or phrases that signal general information.

  In general, … Overall, … On the whole, …

🎧 **2.1** Listen to *Food waste*. Complete the sentences with the signal the speaker uses before each main idea.

1 _____ just because it looks bad, they throw it out rather than use it.

2 _____ not all supermarkets are bad …

3 _____ I think we need to focus on a bigger problem: the environment …

4 _____ it stops the heat from escaping from the atmosphere and causes the greenhouse effect, which causes global warming, but I didn't know it was more damaging than carbon dioxide.

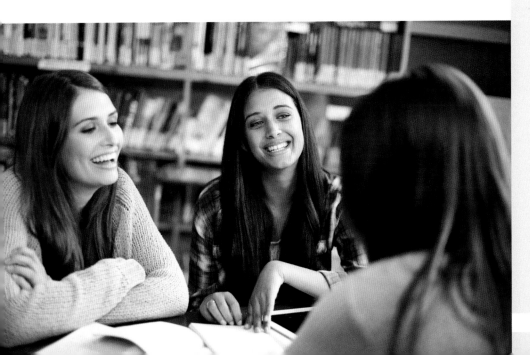

Listening for additional information

D Close listening

1 🎧 **2.2** Listen to the first part of *Food waste*. Match the speaker to the correct question.

> Amira   Julia   Sofia

1 Who wants to eat fewer apples? _____
2 Who is going to be careful when choosing food? _____
3 Who is worried about supermarket waste? _____

2 🎧 **2.3** Listen to the rest of *Food waste*. Choose the correct letter, A, B, or C to complete the sentences.

1 The profit that supermarkets make on produce is
   A 50%   B 15%   C 20%.

2 The cost of food wasted a year is
   A $13.1 billion   B $130 million   C $133 billion.

3 The largest proportion of landfill sites is made up of
   A paper and   B food waste   C household
      packaging   trash.

4 According to the students, the most damaging greenhouse gas is
   A methane   B carbon dioxide C oxygen.

5 The students discuss the following week's lecture about
   A world hunger   B wasted food   C global warming.

E Critical thinking

Discuss these questions in a group.

1 What types of food do you usually throw out? Why?
   I sometimes throw out … because …

2 Does your country have an environmental problem due to wasted food? Can you think of any countries that do?
   I think / don't think my country has an … as / because, …

3 Imagine you had to keep all the food you bought for a month. How do you think you could use up all the food so that there is nothing wasted at the end of the month?

Study skills   Optimal learning to suit you

Learning is easier and more effective when:

… the material suits you.

Take action to ensure that:

• you are on a course you find interesting and relevant.
• the material you use is at the right level.

… you combine technologies to suit you: use face-to-face methods solely, or in combination with technology, where you find this helps learning.

… the time is right.

• at the best time of day or night to suit your learning.
• when you have no distractions.
• when your time is well planned to make the study session interesting.
• when you can learn at your own pace.

© Stella Cottrell (2013)

1   Read *Optimal learning to suit you* and answer these questions with a partner.

1   What do you find interesting about your course?

2   What background knowledge did you have before you started the course?

3   What materials do you use for your course? Are they paper-based or do they involve technology such as a computer?

4   Do you prefer practicing with printed materials or with technology-based activities? Why?

5   When do you study—during the day or at night? Why is this best for you?

6   What types of things distract you when you are studying? How do you avoid them?

2   Complete the sentences. Then compare your ideas with a partner.

1   A good student is someone who …

2   A good course book is one that …

3   A good time to study is when …

4   A good place to study is where …

5   Technology is good for learning when …

6   Courses that are the most interesting are those that …

Brain food

A Vocabulary preview

1   Read the sentences and circle the best definition for the words in bold.

1   Some foods can help improve your **concentration**, which could be helpful when you listen to long lectures.

a   ability to focus your attention   b   ability to stay awake

2   One way to do better in school is to regularly eat **brain food**.

a   food that helps you think   b   food that helps you move

3   There are some foods you should **avoid** because they have few or no health benefits.

a   never use   b   use often

4   If you want to stay healthy, there are several factors to **consider** when choosing what to eat.

a   think about   b   do quickly

5   Drinking caffeine has an **impact** on how long you can stay focused.

a   benefit   b   effect

6   Eating breakfast before school is **recommended**.

a   not allowed   b   a good idea

7   The effects from caffeine are only **temporary**.

a   last for a short period of time   b   last forever

8   Eating foods cooked in a lot of oil has the **potential** to cause serious health problems.

a   danger   b   possibility

2   **Work with a partner. Which of the statements from Exercise 1 do you agree with?**

B Before you listen

Activating prior knowledge

Answer these questions with a partner.

1   Look at the picture on page 33. How does the brain in the image look different from a normal brain?

2   Look at the image again. What do you think the lecturer is going to talk about?

C Global listening

Making predictions about what you will hear will help you understand what the speaker is trying to say. Making predictions also helps you anticipate vocabulary and develop ideas about the topic. There are several strategies you can use to make predictions.

- Notice the title or key words and turn them into a question

  Title: *Brain food*   Question: *What is brain food?*

- Think about the topic and ask yourself questions that you can answer about it

What do you already know about the topic? Or what do you want to know about the topic?

Try to answer the *Wh-* questions the discussion or lecture might address.

1 You are going to hear a radio interview about brain food. Work with a partner and make predictions before you listen.

   1 Why do you think some foods are known as "brain food"?
   2 What are some examples of brain food?
   3 What are the benefits of eating brain food?

2 🎧 2.4 Listen to *Brain food* and check which of your predictions were correct.

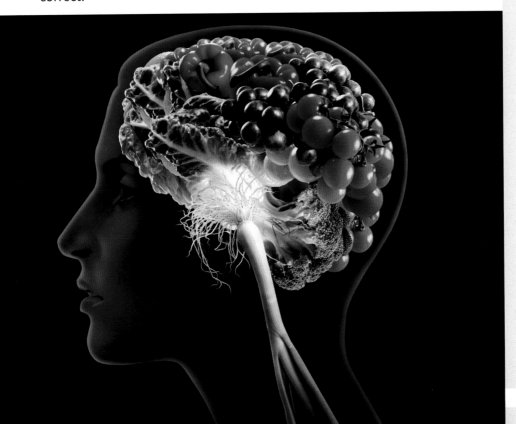

D Close listening

1 🎧 **2.5** Listen to some excerpts from *Brain food* and match the food with its benefits.

1 chocolate   a can improve learning

2 blueberries   b can help the heart

3 fish   c can help you focus

2 🎧 **2.4** Listen again and circle the best answer to complete the sentences.

1 Coffee and chocolate have **similar** / **different** benefits.

2 The **memory** / **heart** benefits when someone consumes sugar.

3 The benefits from sugar and chocolate last for a **short** / **long** time.

4 People should avoid too much **chocolate** / **fish**.

5 The doctor recommends **milk** / **dark** chocolate.

6 Memory is better after a healthy **breakfast** / **lunch**.

7 Brain foods **can** / **cannot** raise your IQ.

E Critical thinking

Discuss these questions in a group.

1 Do you eat any of the brain foods mentioned in the listening text? Which ones? Why do you eat them?

I eat some of the brain foods mentioned in listening text. I eat …

I eat these foods because I think they …

2 What differences do you see in yourself when you consume brain food versus when you don't?

When I eat brain food, I feel more / less …

It doesn't affect me because …

3 What impact do you think food has on intelligence?

I believe food makes you …

I'm not sure it has much impact because …

Pronunciation for listening

Stress in phrasal verbs

Phrasal verbs are very common in spoken English. These are fixed phrases formed with a verb and a preposition or adverb, which when combined has a particular meaning.

The main stress in phrasal verbs is usually found within the verb.

make up

ap*prove* of

Three-part phrasal verbs stress the main verb and first particle.

walk out on

1 🎧 **2.6** Listen to these sentences from *Food waste* and *Brain food*. Write the missing preposition or adverb on the lines.

1 I'd like to point _____ that cereals aren't just good for your mental health.

2 I know a lot of your students look forward _____ snacking on chocolate candy in the afternoon.

3 Researchers have also found _____ that caffeine can help improve your concentration.

4 Now, moving _____ from chocolate, I've always heard that fish is brain food.

5 Caffeine can be considered a brain food because it helps you wake _____.

6 I can't believe they throw _____ fruit and vegetables that are imperfect.

7 I was thinking _____ the apples I buy every day.

2 🎧 **2.7** Underline the phrasal verbs. Circle the syllable(s) that should be stressed. Then listen and check.

1 The instructor moved on from the small talk and focused on the lecture about wasted food.

2 The substitute is going to take over while the instructor is away at a conference on food waste.

3 Juan Pablo never runs away from a challenge and he is going to find a solution for all the food waste in the cafeteria.

4 Angelina tried to get ahead of the food waste problem by looking for a solution before the university declared it an issue.

Vocabulary development

Phrasal verbs

There are hundreds of phrasal verbs used in spoken English. When the individual parts of a phrasal verb are used together, the phrase has a very individual meaning. Compare:

catch = stop and hold onto sb / sth

catch up = to talk to someone you haven't seen in a while and find out what they have been doing

Base verbs can combine with more than one particle (a preposition or an adverb). The particle changes the meaning of the phrasal verb.

talk + about = discuss   *talk + into* = convince

Many phrasal verbs cannot be separated, and must always appear in a sentence as verb + particle + object.

count + on + me

You can count on me to help if you need advice.

However, there are also phrasal verbs where the object falls between the verb and particle: verb + object + particle.

let + me + down

I know my father will not let me down when I call him for advice.

1   Match the phrasal verbs in bold with the correct definitions.

1	**point out**	a	discover
2	**give up**	b	get rid of something
3	**turn into**	c	rise from bed after sleeping
4	**get up**	d	become
5	**throw out**	e	show
6	**find out**	f	quit

2   Complete the questions with a phrasal verb from Exercise 1.

1   Do you _____ at the same time every day?

2   What is one thing you would find difficult to _____ from your life completely?

3   If you could _____ a famous person, who would it be? Why?

4   What would you _____ to a person visiting your city for the first time?

5   What could you _____ to make your room cleaner?

6   What do you wish you could _____ from your textbooks?

3   Ask and answer the questions from Exercise 2 with a partner.

Academic words

1 Match the words in bold with the correct definitions.

1 Angelica's **strategy** was to finish college and then go to graduate school in order to get a management position with a good company.

2 The presidential candidates had a **debate** to allow voters to hear their opinions on certain issues.

3 There is some **evidence** that people are living longer.

4 The scientists presented their **statistics** in a bar graph that made it easy to understand all the numbers.

5 Doctors questioned his **mental** health because he was having trouble remembering things.

6 People who run marathons are usually in good **physical** shape from all of their training.

7 School advisors encourage students to **participate** in extra activities in order to improve their chances of getting into a good university.

8 I know Sibyl is going to **react** with surprise when she learns she actually won the science fair.

a _____ (n) group of numbers that represent facts

b _____ (v) behave in a particular way because of something that is happening

c _____ (n) discussion in which people state different opinions

d _____ (n) plan or method for achieving something

e _____ (n) facts that help to prove something

f _____ (adj) relating to the body

g _____ (v) to take part in something

h _____ (adj) existing in the mind

2 Answer these questions with a partner.

1 Do you think it's important to have better mental health or better physical health? Why?

2 How do you react when you hear bad news? When you hear good news?

3 Can you give any evidence or provide any statistics to support an idea you have about dieting?

4 What benefits are there to eating healthy food?

5 Discuss a good strategy for improving someone's diet.

Speaking model

You are going to learn about defining relative clauses, giving advice and suggestions, and pronouncing consonant blends. You are then going to use this to give advice on how food waste can be reduced in your area.

A Analyze

Complete the talk with the phrases in the box.

> to clean up the streets   there are over 100,000 inhabitants
> the things they don't want   providing more waste bins

Hello, today I'm going to present my advice for the local government planning committee about how to reduce the amount of litter people leave on the streets in my town of Kimperley. Statistics show that Kimperley, where [1]_____, has a waste problem. In fact, there is evidence that it has the biggest waste problem in the state. People often leave their litter, that is, [2]_____, on the streets. Last weekend, when I was walking downtown, I saw five people throw things away on the streets. I think the committee should do more to get residents to participate in cleaning up the streets. One suggestion is that the committee sends everyone in the area information and advice in the mail, so that they can learn about the damage to the environment caused by waste. How about [3]_____ on the streets to encourage people to use them, too? Finally, I recommend the committee employs more people [4]_____ more regularly. These are my top three recommendations.

B Discuss

1   Does your town have a litter problem like Kimperley?

2   Do you agree with the speaker's suggestions to reduce Kimperley's litter problem?

3   Can you think of any other ways the Kimperley local government planning committee could stop people from throwing litter on the streets?

Grammar

Relative clauses

Defining relative clauses are parts of sentences that add extra, essential information about a noun. Relative pronouns are used to connect a relative clause to its noun. The most common are *who, when, which,* and *that*. However, we can also use *whose, when,* and *where*.

*There's someone in my class **whose** <u>parents are famous</u>.*

*Last month was **when** <u>the latest smartphone came out</u>.*

*The room **where** <u>we met for the discussion was quiet</u>.*

If the relative pronoun refers to the object of the sentence, we can remove it.

England is the country ~~where~~ I'd most like to visit.

If the relative clause is adding more information to the sentence that is not essential, we can separate the clause with commas. This is called a non-defining relative clause.

The professor, ~~whose job it was to grade the tests,~~ awarded most students a good grade.

1 Underline the relative clauses in the sentences.

　1　The last time we saw each other was <u>when we were in Mrs. Kingston's class</u>.

　2　The store where I usually buy my stationery is closed.

　3　The man, whose job it is to fix the computers, hasn't finished.

　4　The students, whose grades were very low, had to retake the test.

　5　Two thousand sixteen was when I graduated school.

　6　I remember the day when I got my exam grades. I was very nervous.

2 Look again at Exercise 1 and remove any of the relative pronouns if they refer to the object of the sentence.

3 Combine the sentences using a relative clause. Use commas where necessary.

　1　The woman's job is to order books. She is a library assistant.

　　_____

　2　Eduardo's exam is tomorrow. He is studying.

　　_____

　3　Last week we did the experiment. It failed.

　　_____

　4　Spain can get very hot in the summer. It's a popular tourist destination.

　　_____

Speaking skill

> You can use the following phrases to offer advice or suggestions to others.
>
> Sometimes we use the *-ing* form of the verb:
>
> *I suggest eating a good breakfast in the morning.*
>
> *How about getting a pet bird to take care of?*
>
> *I'd recommend reading a good book to help you relax.*
>
> Others are followed by the infinitive:
>
> *One idea is to volunteer in your free time.*
>
> *It might be a good idea to eat vegetables at every meal.*
>
> Another common way to offer advice is using the modal verb *should*. *Should* is always followed by the base form of the verb.
>
> *You should always eat three meals a day. Skipping meals is not good for you.*

GLOSSARY

compost (n) a mixture of decaying plants and vegetables that is added to soil to improve its quality

imperfect (adj) not perfect, with bad qualities

landfill (n) a large hole in the ground where waste from people's homes is buried

1 Correct the mistakes in these sentences.

   1 One idea is to donating more food to charities.

   2 I'd recommend avoid eating too much food in the evening.

   3 How about to buy imperfect fruit at the market?

   4 It might be a good idea save food from ending up in the landfills.

   5 I suggest use leftover food for compost or to feed farm animals.

   6 You should buying food from the "ugly" section of the market.

2 Complete the dialogues with advice and suggestions.

   1 A: I really need to find a job.

      B: I suggest _____.

   2 A: I don't know what subject to major in.

      B: How about _____?

   3 A: I'm finding it difficult to sleep.

      B: It might be a good idea to _____.

   4 A: I want to improve my diet.

      B: I'd recommend_____.

3 Work in a small group. Take turns asking for advice for the situations. The rest of the group should give advice.

   1 You are worried about your diet.

   2 You are feeling sad after taking a test.

   3 Your study group needs to choose a topic for a project in health class.

4 Listen to the group and choose the best advice for each problem.

Pronunciation for speaking

> ## Consonant clusters
>
> Consonant clusters are groups of consonants in words that are pronounced very quickly together, e.g., *br* in *break*. Many of these consonant clusters fall at the beginning of a word.
>
> Common clusters in English are *bl-, br-, cl-, cr-, fl-, fr-, gl-,* and *gr-*.
>
> | | |
> |---|---|
> | *blue* | *brew* |
> | *clue* | *crew* |
> | *flee* | *free* |
> | *glass* | *grass* |

1 🎧 **2.8** Listen to the following words. Underline the word you hear. Then listen again and repeat.

1	clue	crew
2	blaze	braise
3	flame	frame
4	fly	fry
5	flee from	free from
6	green glasses	green grasses
7	clean room	green room
8	blue tea	brew tea

2 Say the words from Exercise 1 to a partner. Can your partner identify which words you are saying?

3 Create two sentences using one or more of the consonant clusters in the box.

bl-	br-	cl-	cr-	fl-	fr-	gl-	gr-

*The body sometimes wants **fried** foods, but the **brain** wants healthy **fresh fruit**.*

1 _____

2 _____

4 Answer these questions with a partner.

1 Do you prefer French fries or fresh fruit? Why?

2 Have you ever been blamed for something you didn't do? What was it?

3 What are your favorite clothing items?

4 What does your country's flag look like?

Speaking task

Present advice on ways to reduce food waste in your local town.

Brainstorm

1 Look at this list of ideas. Which do you think would be easy to do in your town? Mark from 1 = very easy to 8 = very difficult.

___ buy imperfect fruit and vegetables

___ offer free food-waste seminars

___ donate leftover food to local food banks

___ offer rewards for people who don't throw away any food at local restaurants

___ provide wasted food to be used as compost

___ buy less food to reduce the amount you throw away

___ offer a training plan for residents to learn more about how to use leftover food

___ set up trash cans with separate areas for landfill trash and compost

2 Work with a partner to add two more ideas.

1 _____

2 _____

Plan

Decide on the two best ideas from the list, plus one of your own suggestions. Write some notes giving advice to the local government planning committee based on these ideas. Support your ideas with examples.

Speak

Present your advice to a partner. Remember to use language for offering advice and suggestions and relative clauses.

Share

Work with a new partner. Talk about the presentation you listened to. Decide whether you would change anything you talked about. Say why.

Reflect

Think about your own behavior. What can you can do to reduce food waste in your town?

Review

Wordlist

MACMILLAN DICTIONARY

Vocabulary preview

agriculture (n) **	consider (v) ***	recommended (v) ***
avoid (v) ***	feed (v) ***	solution (n) ***
billion (n) **	hunger (n) *	temporary (adj) ***
brain food (phrase)	impact (n) ***	waste (n) ***
challenge (n) ***	potential (adj) ***	
concentration (n) ***	profit (n) ***	

Vocabulary development

find out (phr v)	give up (phr v)	throw out (phr v)
get up (phr v)	point out (phr v)	turn into (phr v)

Academic words

debate (n) ***	participate (v) **	statistics (n)
evidence (n) ***	physical (adj) ***	strategy (n) ***
mental (adj) ***	react (v) **	

Academic words review

Complete the sentences using the words in the box.

debate   labels   normal   physical   statistics

1   A serious discussion is often called a _____.
2   If you want to know what chemicals are in your food, read the _____ on the packets!
3   To make sure the competitors were fit enough for the race, they all had to have a _____ examination.
4   It is important to present _____ in a way that is easy for people to understand and interpret.
5   In many countries the _____ working day is from 9:00 a.m. to 5:00 p.m.

Unit review

Listening 1	☐	I can listen for important information.
Listening 2	☐	I can make predictions about what I am going to hear.
Study skill	☐	I can use strategies for optimal learning.
Vocabulary	☐	I can use a range of phrasal verbs.
Grammar	☐	I can use relative clauses.
Speaking	☐	I can offer advice and make suggestions.

Discussion point

Discuss with a partner.

1 Have you had a job or any paid work before? Did you like it? Why / why not?

I worked at … I liked it because …

2 Which of the office spaces in the infographic is normal in your country?

In my country, offices are usually …

3 What kind of work do you want to do when you finish school? What do you think the office space will be like?

I would like to … I think the office would be …

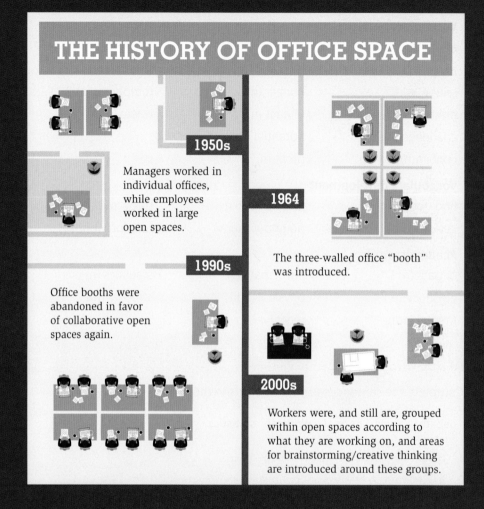

THE HISTORY OF OFFICE SPACE

1950s

Managers worked in individual offices, while employees worked in large open spaces.

1964

The three-walled office "booth" was introduced.

1990s

Office booths were abandoned in favor of collaborative open spaces again.

2000s

Workers were, and still are, grouped within open spaces according to what they are working on, and areas for brainstorming/creative thinking are introduced around these groups.

VIDEO

QUIET SPACES

Before you watch

Answer the questions with a partner.

1 Are you the kind of person who prefers a busy city or the peace of the countryside?

2 Do you prefer to work and study with music or in silence? Why?

3 Have you ever had to share a bedroom or work space with anyone? What was it like?

UNIT AIMS

LISTENING 1 Listening for reasons
LISTENING 2 Listening for contrasts
STUDY SKILL Getting the most out of discussion

VOCABULARY Business vocabulary
GRAMMAR Modal verbs for advice
SPEAKING Presentation on teamwork

Aerial view of people working in an office in London, U.K.

While you watch

1 Work with a partner and predict the order that you will see these things.

___ a she uses an app on her phone to choose an office

___ b a man says all the things you can use the office for

___ c a busy street in New York City

___ d you see a sign with rules about using the office

___ e she finds the building and opens the office door

2 Watch the video and check your answers.

After you watch

Answer the questions with a partner.

1 Is it a good idea to rent an office for an hour? Why / why not?

2 How do you like to "take a breather" from work or studies?

3 What would you do if you rented an office and your neighbor was incredibly noisy?

Work space

A Vocabulary preview

1 Match the words in bold with the correct definitions.

1 Unhealthy food has a bad **effect** on the human body.

2 **I guess** you can take the advanced class, but it will be hard.

3 Juan Carlos and Eduardo **seem** to like science because they are taking three classes.

4 My advisor **set up** a meeting to talk about my classes next semester.

5 After the movie, the doors opened and people began to **emerge** onto the street.

6 Mikhail works in a **cubicle** at his company; he decorated it with pictures of his family.

7 The desk **height** was too tall; Frederik couldn't reach it.

8 He worked very hard on his project and the **result** was an A on his report card.

a saying something you think is probably true

b organize or plan something

c appear to be something

d a change

e a small enclosed area that has thin walls

f the final product

g come out of something

h the degree to which something is high or someone is tall

2 Complete the sentences with the correct form of the words from Exercise 1.

1 Some students _____ to think that they do not need to study to succeed.

2 Burik's _____ had a desk and chair. He took some pictures and a plant to decorate it.

3 _____ I like studying in the library best because it is so quiet.

4 Workers began to _____ from their cubicles before the 3:00 meeting.

5 Chen _____ a doctor's appointment for Friday at 4:00.

6 The flood was the _____ of the large amounts of rain.

7 My boss and I aren't the same _____. He's a lot taller than me!

8 Angela's good grades had an _____ on her college admissions.

B Before you listen

Activating prior knowledge

Look at the picture on page 47. Work with a partner and discuss these questions.

1 Look at the picture of an office with cubicles. Have you ever seen an office like this? Where?

2 Is this kind of office space common in your country? If not, what do offices normally look like?

3 What kind of office space would you prefer to work in? Why?

C Global listening

 3.1 Listen to *Work space*. Number the topics 1–6 in the order in which you hear them.

___ closed offices   ___ cubicles

___ combination of office space   ___ shared spaces

___ desks   ___ open-plan spaces

Listening for reasons

D Close listening

Speakers will often support their ideas with reasons. When listening, it's useful to note reasons speakers provide as these help you to understand the speaker's views. Listen for signal words that point to reasons.

The reason is that I read a lot about cubicles.

*You wouldn't want everyone to hear about those things. **Because of this,** I think closed offices are the better option.*

*In fact, research shows that employees in open-plan offices are more confident in sharing their ideas. **Therefore / Consequently,** they are better communicators.*

1 🎧 3.1 Listen to *Work space* again. According to the speakers, which of these is a reason to support an open or closed office space? Write *O* (Open) or *C* (Closed).

   1 good for large groups ____

   2 better for private discussions with managers ____

   3 better for increased teamwork ____

   4 easier to ask questions ____

   5 better for ideas ____

2 🎧 3.1 Listen again. Write the advantages and disadvantages in the correct space in the table.

	Open office space	Closed office space
Advantages	fit more [1] _____ costs [2] _____	[5] _____ get more ideas [6] _____ noise [7] _____ privacy
Disadvantages	[3] _____ distractions [4] _____ privacy	[8] _____ expensive can't work [9] _____ as easily

E Critical thinking

Discuss these questions in a group.

1 Some professionals, for example doctors and lawyers, don't work in open-plan offices. Why? Do you think they should?

2 Should a boss have a separate office from his / her employees? Why / why not?

Study skills — Getting the most out of discussion

Before

Ensure you have done any tasks agreed for the group.

Do some background reading. Think about it.

What questions do you have?

During

Check that everyone can see and hear everyone else.

Be open to hearing something new.

Note down useful information.

If you don't understand something, ask.

Link what you hear to what you already know.

Contribute, e.g., by raising points that interest you.

After

Go over your notes and summarize them. Add any new details.

Check that you know exactly when you will do activities arising out of the group. Are they in your diary?

© Stella Cottrell (2013)

1 Answer these questions with a partner.

1 Why is it important to do things before, during, and after a discussion?

2 What is a discussion you recently participated in? Did you use any of the points from the box to participate more effectively?

2 Complete the sentences. Then compare your ideas with a partner.

1 It is important to do some background reading on the subject because …

2 You need to hear and see everyone else because …

3 Useful information to note includes …

4 It is good to link what you hear to what you already know because …

5 You can make contributions by raising points that interest you or by …

6 You should go over and summarize your notes after a lecture because …

A big business

A Vocabulary preview

1 Match the words in bold with the correct definitions.

1	**achievement** (n)	a	a particular thing you did well
2	**allow** (v)	b	a relationship between people who are friends
3	**create** (v)	c	to start a new system or process
4	**efficient** (adj)	d	works well
5	**friendship** (n)	e	to give someone or something the time or opportunity to do something
6	**introduce** (v)		
7	**part-time** (adj)	f	make something new or original
8	**sales** (n)	g	the process of selling goods or services for money
		h	done for only a part of the time

2 Complete the sentences with the correct form of the words in Exercise 1.

1 Michael graduated from college. His parents are having a party to celebrate this _____.

2 The president will _____ his new economic policy to the media today.

3 The company is doing very well; it will _____ many new jobs for the community.

4 Workers in closed office spaces work harder and are more _____ than those in open offices.

5 I work _____ so I only come in to the office two days a week.

6 You form many _____ at work and they can last the rest of your life.

7 I work in _____ so it's my job to sell my company's products to the public.

8 Some companies _____ you to leave early when you need to go to the doctor's.

3 Discuss these questions with a partner.

1 What is your greatest achievement?

2 Is it a good idea to form a friendship with your boss?

3 Why do some people choose to work part-time?

B Before you listen

1 Answer the questions with a partner.

1 What big companies can you think of? What are some things they have in common?

One of the largest companies in my country is …

Most big companies have things like …

2 What are some benefits a big company can offer workers?

2 Look at the picture. What do you know about the company?

C Global listening

🎧 **3.2** Listen to *A big business* and circle the correct answer.

1 Who started Starbucks?

  a doctors   b students   c customers

2 How many workers does Starbucks have at its headquarters?

  a over 3,000   b over 3,200   c over 3,500

3 What is something Starbucks is known for?

  a openness   b holiday pay   c hot food

4 Which of these benefits is something Starbucks does not offer its employees?

  a tuition fees   b healthcare benefits   c free travel to work

5 What kind of employees does Starbucks provide health benefits to?

  a full-time   b part-time   c both full-time and part-time

D Close listening

English has 20 spoken vowel sounds but only five vowel letters. In some words, different vowels can sound very similar. For example:

[ɪ] and [iː]	*live*	*leave*
[ɪ] and [e]	*miss*	*mess*
[e] and [æ]	*set*	*sat*
[æ] and [ʌ]	*fan*	*fun*
[u] and [ju]	*cool*	*cute*

1 🎧 3.3 Listen to four sentences from *A big business*. Circle the word you hear.

1 a live   b leave
2 a eats   b its
3 a each   b itch
4 a mutter   b matter

2 🎧 3.2 Listen to *A big business* again. Complete the flowchart of the presentation. Write no more than two words or a number for each answer.

Big business example: Starbucks

Started in Seattle, WA (U.S.) in [1] _____

Currently has over 3,500 [2] _____ in main office in Seattle.

If company cares about workers, then they care about [3] _____ and the company succeeds.

The company tries to encourage [4] _____—colleagues talk to one another. This leads to good [5] _____ and should then increase sales.

Benefits: The company offers [6] _____ to both part-time and full-time workers. It also helps pay for tuition and learning—through its College [7] _____ Plan.

E Critical thinking

1 Can you think of any other things companies could do to make employees feel happier and motivated at work?

Companies could help employees to … / give / offer employees …

2 Which of your answers to Question 1 would make you want to work at a company? Why?

… would make me want to work at a company, even if they didn't have …

Pronunciation for listening

Continuing speech

Many statements have falling intonation which shows that the speaker has finished speaking.

Starbucks started in 1971.

However, speakers can use rising intonation at the end of statements to let listeners know they are going to continue because they have something to add to what they were saying. For example, when speakers give a list, each item will have rising intonation to let the listener know that more items will be listed.

… if the company cared about its workers, then the workers would care

about the customers and this results in company success.

1 🎧 **3.4** Listen to the sentences from *A big business*. Does the intonation rise or fall? Circle the correct answer.

   1   rise   fall

   2   rise   fall

   3   rise   fall

   4   rise   fall

2 🎧 **3.4** Listen again and repeat the sentences.

3 Answer these questions with a partner. Use the techniques you have learned on rising and falling intonation.

   1   What are three of your favorite classes? Why?

       I like English because the teacher is a lot of fun, math

       because it's really useful, and gym because I love soccer.

   2   Talk about three jobs you would like to have.

   3   Now talk about three reasons for taking each of those jobs.

Vocabulary development

Business vocabulary

1 Match the words in bold with the correct definitions.

1	**annual** (adj)	a	happening once a year
2	**bi-annual** (adj)	b	twice as much of something
3	**double** (adj)	c	done twice a year
4	**quantity** (n)	d	the amount of something
5	**realistic** (adj)	e	not having work or income
6	**suggestion** (n)	f	three times as much of something
7	**triple** (adj)	g	an idea or plan for changing things
8	**unemployment** (n)	h	based on facts and situations as they really are

2 Underline the best words to complete the text.

I want to start my own business. I talked to my business teacher and asked him for help. He gave me a good ¹ **suggestion / quantity**. His tip was to learn more about corporate culture. He said that I need to be ² **double / realistic** and know what happens in other companies. He also said that I might not make much and it will take a long time before I can ³ **double / quantity** my money. He told me that my employees have to feel safe. They don't want to worry about ⁴ **suggestions / unemployment**. I asked what skills I need and he suggested a great tip: my special skill should be making the workplace open, friendly, and diverse. I'm going to take some classes about managing people. Then hopefully I'll make ⁵ **bi-annual / triple** the money every year! I think that's very ⁶ **unemployment / realistic**.

Academic words

1   Match the words in bold with the correct definitions.

1   The writing teacher will ask for a **revision** of your paper to help improve it.

a   a first draft   b   a second draft

2   Things are always **evolving**. You never know what will happen next.

a   staying the same   b   changing

3   The homework was to write a **paragraph** on business growth.

a   one sentence   b   a block of more than one sentence

4   My results **indicate** that recycling helps improve the environment.

a   show   b hide

5   Presidents of large companies often have to introduce a new **policy** to make things run smoothly.

a   possible idea   b   a set of plans

6   Mark isn't very **academic**. He usually gets low grades on his exams.

a   not good at school   b   good at school

7   There is a **definite** connection between exercising and losing weight.

a   certain   b   unclear

8   The teacher said to **specify** the date I plan to finish my project.

a   say exactly   b   say approximately

2   Complete these sentences with the correct word from Exercise 1.

1   In general, the exam results at my school _____ a successful academic year.

2   The lawyer asked the client to _____ the date that the accident happened.

3   Ideas are always _____, especially in businesses where employees talk often.

4   We have not chosen a _____ date for our trip, but we will come sometime this summer.

5   My project needed a lot of _____ because the first draft was not very good.

6   The class is going to have an _____ discussion on the benefits of open-plan office spaces.

7   There is a new lateness _____ in the company—new rules were needed.

8   The _____ in that book on environmental issues is very interesting.

Speaking model

You are going to learn about giving advice, pronunciation patterns, and taking turns. You are then going to discuss and present solutions to a business problem.

A Model

1   Read the notes and choose the best word to complete the summary of the problem below.

- *Julio & Marcus—working together in sales for a large company*
- *Julio: always late, poor work quality, tired, leaves early—work not finished*
- *Marcus: needs to finish Julio's work, frustrated—they earn the same. "It's unfair!"*
- *Julio: reason for bad performance—wife had a baby, not getting enough sleep*
- *anger, communication problems between both men*
- *work not finished, sales are down, company is losing money*

Julio and Marcus are part of a [1] **sales / marketing** team of a large company. Julio's work is much [2] **better / worse** than Marcus'. As a result, the team has [3] **communication / technical** problems and is making [4] **more / less** money.

2   Read the presentation the student gave to solve this problem. Circle the language the student uses to give advice.

Good morning. My presentation today is about how Julio and Marcus can improve their relationship at work so that they can start making more money for the business. Julio said that the reason why he is having problems at work because he has a family. However, this is not realistic. A lot of people have evolving family lives and they still have to work. People need to be able to balance their work lives with their family lives. Julio and Marcus need to find a way to work together. One suggestion is that they have a split schedule. In other words, Marcus could work earlier in the morning because Julio needs to come in later. Then Julio could work later in the evening. They would then work the same number of hours and Marcus would not be doing double the work. Julio has to take the late shift so that he can sleep later in the morning. I think if they do this, they will both do the same amount of work. They should also specify a time to meet in the middle of each day so that they can make sure they are getting everything done. In conclusion, communicating and changing the schedule would be an easy way to make both of them happy, and help increase company profits. Profits could be checked on a bi-annual basis to make sure this new policy works. Thank you.

B Discuss

Do you think the speaker's solution is good? Can you think of another solution that could work?

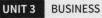

Grammar

Modal verbs for advice

The most common way to give advice in English is by using the verb *should / shouldn't*. You use *should* to talk about things you strongly recommend.

*They **should** specify a time to meet each day.*

*You **shouldn't** forget your homework.*

When offering more than one piece of advice, we use *could*.

*If you feel sick, you **could** go to the doctor or you could stay home and rest.*

You can also use *might* or *may* or *might not / may not*.

*You **may** want to talk to the teacher about ways to improve your English.*

*You **might** not choose to attend review classes, but it's a good idea.*

1 Complete each sentence with *should, shouldn't, may, might,* or *could*. Sometimes more than one option is possible.

1 The CEO said the business plan was confidential. You _____ tell the competitor about it.

2 Ricardo _____ go to medical school or possibly law school. He is smart enough to attend either one.

3 I need to go to the market today, but I'm sick, so I _____ wait until tomorrow.

4 There is a sign on the electrical outlet that says you _____ be careful when you plug things in.

5 Friday is a holiday, so we _____ go to the shopping center or to see a movie.

6 You _____ study if you want to pass the professor's final exam.

7 Suzana _____ volunteer at the hospital because she likes to help people.

8 I want to make new friends. I _____ either join a club or play on a team.

2 Correct the errors in these sentences.

1 We shouldn't make good products.

2 We could selling different types of services.

3 You shouldn't having friendships with your co-workers.

4 You might not wanting to study all weekend. It's up to you.

5 You couldn't study tomorrow, or you could study tonight instead.

6 We should make our employees work in their spare time.

Speaking skill

In order to have a successful conversation, speakers need to take turns. There are certain turn-taking phrases we often use in English to show that we would like to contribute to the conversation:

Before you go on …   *Sorry for interrupting, but …*

Can I say something …   *Let me just say something here …*

There are also phrases we can use to show we would like to go first:

Can I talk first?   *Can I go ahead?*

I'd like to start the discussion by …   *Let me just say …*

If someone interrupts but you are not finished speaking, there are phrases you can use to show you'd like to finish:

Hold on a second, …   *As I was saying …*

I'm almost done …   *If I can return to …*

It is also polite to encourage others to take turns:

I'd like to know what [Juan] thinks …

That's enough from me. What does everyone else think?

1   Match the function in the box to the phrases in bold.

> encouraging others to speak   interrupting   saying you are not finished

> 1   A: We are learning a lot in history this semester and …
>
>   B: **Before you go on**, please remember there is a test next week.
>
> 2   A: The museum has some fabulous paintings. The artist used …
>
>   B: I just thought of something. There is a technology museum …
>
>   A: **Hold on a second!** Then you can tell us about that museum. The artist …
>
> 3   So, I think the best businesses are those that have experienced managers. **That's enough from me. What does everyone else think?**

2   Work with a partner. Use the prompts to have a conversation.

Student A   Say you are starting a new business—explain what it is and who you have employed. When Student B interrupts, re-take control of the conversation politely.

Student B   Interrupt politely and try to give advice about how to make the business better.

3   In the same group, switch roles and try the conversation again.

Pronunciation for speaking

Chunking a presentation

To give an effective presentation, it is important to break your sentences into chunks of language by pausing to allow your audience to understand each part of what you are saying. Pause at periods, commas, and at the end of each piece of information

My presentation today | is about how Julio and Marcus | can improve things at work | so that they can start making more money | for the business. |

When you have chunked your text, try stressing two of the most important words in every chunk to make your point more effective.

My PREsentation toDAY | is about how JUlio and MARcus | can imPROVE things at WORK | so that they can START making more MONey | FOR the BUSiness. |

1 🔊 **3.5** Listen to the model answer and use a pen to chunk the text. Mark where the speaker pauses. The introduction has been done for you.

My presentation today | is about how Julio and Marcus | can improve things at work | so that they can start making more money | for the business.
Julio has said that the reason why he is having problems at work is because he has a family. A lot of people have babies and families and they still have to work.
People need to be able to balance their work lives with their family lives. Julio and Marcus need to establish ways to overcome this. One suggestion is that they have a split schedule. In other words, Marcus could work earlier in the morning because Julio needs to come in later. Then, Julio could work later in the evening.
They would then work the same number of hours and Marcus would not be doing double the work. Julio has to take the late shift so that he can sleep later in the morning. I think if they do this, they will both do the same amount of work. They should also specify a time to meet in the middle of each day so that they can make sure they are getting everything done.
In conclusion, communicating and changing the schedule would be an easy way to make both of them happy, and help increase company profits. Profits could be checked on a bi-annual basis to make sure this new policy works.

2 🔊 **3.5** Listen to the model answer again and mark where the speaker stresses in each chunk.

3 Compare your answer with your partner and take turns reading aloud your model with the pauses and stress.

Speaking task

Work in a small group to present a business plan to turn a failing business around.

Brainstorm

Read the report notes about a car factory called Green Motors.

- Car factory with assembly line
- Workers on assembly line
- Workers taking longer to complete tasks
- Deadlines missed
- Cars breaking down—returned
- No overtime pay
- Long hours
- Employees doing work they weren't trained for
- "Managers are too strict"
- "They don't praise us enough"
- Some employees work harder than others—angry!
- Old equipment, cold factory
- Long commute to/from factory (1h+)
- No health benefits—people work even when sick
- "No communication between employees and managers"

Plan

Work with two other students.

Rank the problems in order of importance considering the overall aim of turning the business around, working together as a team, and improving employee satisfaction.

Choose the biggest three problems and talk about possible solutions.

Decide who is going to talk about each problem and each possible solution.

Speak

Share your opinions about what the biggest problems are and your proposed solutions with another group. Remember to use phrases for turn-taking and modal verbs to offer advice.

Share

Evaluate and discuss the ideas the two groups discussed.

Which group had the most realistic / effective solutions to the problems? Which speakers were effective group members?

Reflect

Discuss the questions with a partner:

Which of the problems Green Motors had would make you feel unhappy at work? Why?

Have you / someone you know ever had any of the above problems at work? What did they do to solve them?

Review

Wordlist

MACMILLAN
DICTIONARY

Vocabulary preview

achievement (n) ***	effect (n) ***	height (n) ***	result (n) ***
allow (v) ***	efficient (adj) ***	I guess (phrase)	sales (n) ***
create (v) ***	emerge (v) ***	introduce (v) ***	seem (v) ***
cubicle (n)	friendship (n) **	part-time (adj) **	set up (v)

Vocabulary development

annual (adj) ***	double (adj) ***	realistic (adj) **	triple (adj) *
bi-annual (adj)	quantity (n) **	suggestion (n) ***	unemployment (n) ***

Academic words

academic (adj) ***	evolve (v) **	paragraph (n) ***	revision (n) **
definite (adj) **	indicate (v) ***	policy (n) ***	specify (v) **

Academic words review

Complete the sentences using the words in the box.

academic	indicate	paragraph	policy	strategy

1 All overseas students who want to study at the university must take an English exam first. It's our _____.

2 The opening _____ of an essay should define the topic.

3 The CEO has announced a new export _____ which he hopes will improve the company's performance.

4 "Are you thinking of going to university, Holly?"
   "I'm not sure. I'm not very _____ and I think I would prefer to get a job."

5 If you want to turn left or right, you must _____ your intention to other drivers.

Unit review

Listening 1		I can listen for the speaker's reasons.
Listening 2		I can distinguish between similar sounds.
Study skill		I can get the most out of a discussion.
Vocabulary		I can use a range of business vocabulary.
Grammar		I can use modal verbs to give advice.
Speaking		I can politely take my turn in a conversation.

4 TRENDS

Discussion point

Discuss with a partner.

1 What kind of phones do you use? Look at the timeline. When was the phone you use the most often invented?

2 Cell phones are owned by one in seven people worldwide. Do you think this figure is higher or lower in your country? Why?

3 When did you first get a cell phone? Why did you get it?

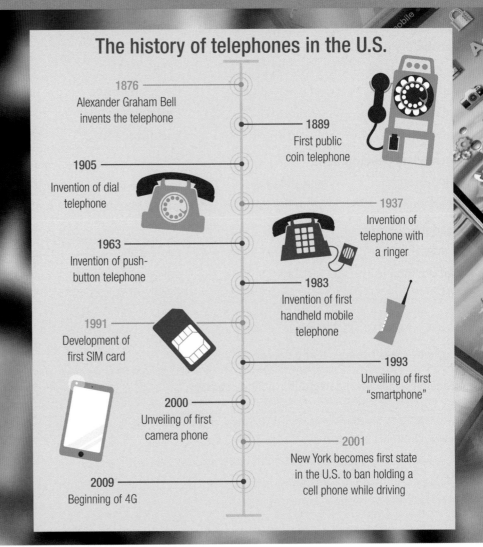

The history of telephones in the U.S.

- **1876** Alexander Graham Bell invents the telephone
- **1889** First public coin telephone
- **1905** Invention of dial telephone
- **1937** Invention of telephone with a ringer
- **1963** Invention of push-button telephone
- **1983** Invention of first handheld mobile telephone
- **1991** Development of first SIM card
- **1993** Unveiling of first "smartphone"
- **2000** Unveiling of first camera phone
- **2001** New York becomes first state in the U.S. to ban holding a cell phone while driving
- **2009** Beginning of 4G

VIDEO

WHO'S TO BLAME?

Before you watch

Match the words in bold with the correct definitions.

1 **autonomous vehicle** (n)
2 **blame** (v)
3 **cause** (n)
4 **motor manufacturers** (n)
5 **to sue someone** (v)

a to say or think that someone or something is responsible

b a company that makes cars

c a vehicle with no driver

d to ask for money in a court of law

e a reason that something, like an accident, happens

UNIT AIMS	LISTENING 1 Listening for dates	VOCABULARY Synonyms and antonyms
	LISTENING 2 Listening for time signals	GRAMMAR Simple past: ordering past events
	STUDY SKILL Time management	SPEAKING Describing a timeline

Modern smartphones.

While you watch

Read the questions. Watch the video and choose the correct answer.

1 Motor manufacturers believe driverless cars will be **less safe** / **safer** than cars with drivers.

2 Driverless cars **will never crash** / **do crash sometimes**.

3 The problem for driverless cars is **normal traffic** / **autonomous cyclists**.

4 If an autonomous vehicle crashes, the manufacturer **might be** / **isn't** to blame.

5 Motor manufacturers study data to discover **the time** / **who or what is to blame** if a crash happens.

After you watch

Answer the questions with a partner.

1 The video says driverless cars will be safer. Do you believe this? Why / why not?

Yes, because …

No, not at all because …

2 What advantages are there to using driverless cars?

3 Would you like to own an autonomous vehicle? Could a bicycle be autonomous? Why / why not?

Car safety

A Vocabulary preview

1 Match the words in bold with the correct definitions.

1	**airbag** (n)	a	a person riding in a car with the driver
2	**anti-lock brake** (n)	b	the back part of something
3	**invent** (v)	c	a device that stops a car without sliding
4	**passenger** (n)	d	make or think of for the first time
5	**rear** (n)	e	a round object that turns and moves a car forward
6	**regulation** (n)	f	a strong device that holds a person in a seat
7	**seat belt** (n)	g	official rule that controls the way things are
8	**wheel** (n)	h	a bag filled with air used to keep a person safe during accidents

2 Complete the sentences with the correct form of the words from Exercise 1.

1 My car holds four people, so I can have three _____.

2 A car with _____ is good if you live in a place with bad winter weather because the car will not slide on ice and snow.

3 When telephones were _____, it changed the way some people live.

4 Bicycles have two _____; a tricycle has three, and a unicycle has only one.

5 The _____ held the passengers in their seats when the flight landed.

6 The U.S. Food and Drug Administration sets the _____ for food safety in the U.S.

7 The _____ in a car will fill with air if the car crashes into another car.

8 Hyun's bedroom is at the _____ of the house, so it is hard for him to hear when someone is at the front door.

3 Discuss these questions with a partner.

1 What has been invented recently? How has it changed your life?

2 What is a regulation at your school that you have to follow? Do you think it should be required or not?

3 Do you have a car? If so, what kind of car do you have? Do you have car insurance?

B Before you listen

Work with a partner. Ask and answer the questions. Then find another classmate. Tell him or her about your first partner.

1   What safety features exist in cars today?
2   Do you take long trips in a car? Why / why not?
3   Is there anything you don't like about driving and / or cars? Why?

   I talked to Michael … He said the common car safety features are … He doesn't like long car rides because …

C Global listening

4.1 Listen to *Car safety.* For question 1, choose three answers (A–E). For question 2, choose two answers (F–J).

1   Which three safety features are mentioned?

   A   speed limits
   B   seat belts
   C   speed cameras
   D   anti-lock brakes
   E   airbags

2   Which two rules and procedures mentioned helped car safety?

   F   inventing new kinds of cars
   G   making every person wear seat belts
   H   copying ideas from airplanes and spaceships
   I   carrying out crash tests to learn about accidents
   J   requiring people to sit down on buses

D Close listening

Listening for dates

> In English, dates are pronounced in certain ways.
>
> To say years, pronounce two whole numbers with a pause in between:
>
> 1991 = nineteen [small pause] ninety-one
>
> When a zero is in the middle, the speaker can say it one of two ways:
>
> 2010 = two thousand [small pause] ten   2010 = twenty [small pause] ten
>
> When a year is a whole number, it is pronounced as such:
>
> 1900 = nineteen hundred   2000 = two thousand

1 🎧 **4.1** Listen to *Car safety* again. Write the dates you hear for each item on the timeline.

Seat belts introduced   Anti-lock brakes introduced   Airbags introduced   First crash test   First car to get a five-star rating

2 🎧 **4.1** Listen again. Choose the correct answer.

1 What is the first idea that is mentioned?
   a   seat belts
   b   air bags
   c   crash tests

2 What was the first vehicle to have anti-lock brakes?
   a   cars
   b   airplanes
   c   buses

3 Where did air bags start?
   a   on the passenger's side
   b   on the driver's side
   c   on both sides

4 What happened to the first car to get only one star?
   a   people still liked it
   b   people started buying it
   c   people thought it was unsafe

E Critical thinking

Discuss these questions in a group.

1 After listening to the text, is your answer to question 1 in *B Before listening* different?

2 Can you add any information about car safety that wasn't in the listening?

3 Imagine you work at car factory and have been asked to think of a new safety feature for a new model. What safety feature would you choose and why?

Study skills | Time management

As only part of your week and year will be timetabled, you will be responsible for organizing most of your study time. This can be challenging when there are commitments such as work, family, and friends.

Organize your time

To manage time well, it helps to do the following:

- be aware of your own time management
- be aware of how much time it takes you to complete each type of study task
- be aware that studying often takes longer than planned for
- schedule time for unexpected events
- schedule time for relaxation and leisure
- be very specific in your time-planning.

© Stella Cottrell (2013)

1   Read *Time management* and answer these questions.

How well do I manage my time now?

Do I usually turn up on time?	Yes	No
Do I keep most appointments?	Yes	No
Do I manage to fit in most of the things that I need to do?	Yes	No
Do I find I often have to do things quickly?	Yes	No
Do I meet deadlines?	Yes	No
Do I have any time to myself to relax?	Yes	No
Do I use my time effectively?	Yes	No

2   Complete this checklist to help you decide which tasks are more important. Then compare your list with a partner.

Have you:

- [ ] written a list of everything you have to do?
- [ ] underlined essential tasks in one color, and items that can wait in another color?
- [ ] identified the most urgent item on the list?
- [ ] figured out the best order in which to do things?
- [ ] figured out how long you can spend on each?
- [ ] entered each essential task into your schedule and planner?

Urban sprawl

A Vocabulary preview

1 Match the words in bold with the correct definitions.

1	**ancient** (adj)	a	all the people who live in an area
2	**forward** (adv)	b	happening a short time ago
3	**loan** (n)	c	inside a period of time
4	**particular** (adj)	d	near or all around a place
5	**population** (n)	e	money borrowed for a specific reason
6	**recent** (adj)	f	in the direction in front of a person
7	**surrounding** (adj)	g	relating to one specific person or thing
8	**within** (prep)	h	very old

2 Read the sentences. Choose *T* (True) or *F* (False) for each sentence.

1 The Coliseum in Rome is ancient.   T / F
2 When you move forward, you are walking toward the back
of something.   T / F
3 You do not have to return the money from a loan.   T / F
4 There is no one particular way that everyone should study.   T / F
5 The population of China is very large.   T / F
6 Anything that happened before the year 1900 is recent.   T / F
7 When you visit a new city, it's a good idea to explore the
surrounding area, too.   T / F
8 People usually board airplanes within five minutes of the
plane leaving.   T / F

B Before you listen

1 What big cities can you think of? What are some common features of big cities?

One big city I can think of is …

Big cities all have …

2 The Burgess model explains a typical city structure. Label the areas using the words in the box.

central business district	inner city	inner suburbs	outer suburbs

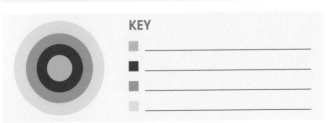

KEY

■ _____

■ _____

■ _____

■ _____

GLOSSARY

suburbs (n) an area or town near a large city but away from its center, where there are many houses

C Global listening

🎧 **4.2** Listen to the lecture *Urban sprawl* and circle the correct date.

1 When did urban sprawl begin?
   a the 1950s
   b almost 3,000 years ago
   c the early 1900s

2 When did urban sprawl start to affect the United States?
   a in 1918
   b in the early 1900s
   c in 1920

3 When did urban sprawl continue to become a problem?
   a in the 1970s
   b in the 1980s
   c in the 1990s

Listening for main ideas

GLOSSARY

affordable (adj) cheap enough for ordinary people to buy

middle-class (adj) the social class that consists mostly of educated people who have professional jobs

phenomenon (n) an event or situation that happens or exists

spread (v) to affect or cover a larger area

urban sprawl (n) when the population of a city spreads to surrounding areas

D Close listening

Listening for time signals

Speakers often use time signals, especially when they are giving the history or timeline of events. Sometimes the times are specific and easy to hear:

In the twentieth century, … During the 1970s, … After x years, …

Sometimes other signal words are used that give you a sense of the time:

after, before, during, later, now, soon, then, today, tomorrow, yesterday

Timelines are a good note-taking tool to make a visual record of dates. You can write notes about the events above or below the dates.

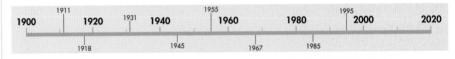

1 🎧 **4.2** Listen to *Urban sprawl* again. Write notes on the timeline.

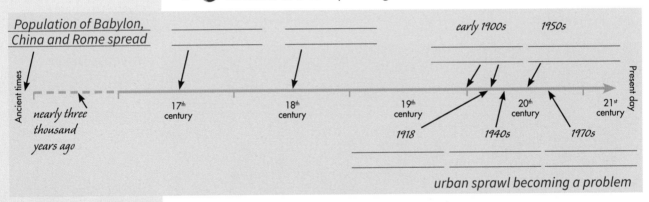

Population of Babylon, China and Rome spread _____ _____ *early 1900s* *1950s*

Ancient times

nearly three thousand years ago

17th century 18th century 19th century 20th century 21st century Present day

1918 *1940s* *1970s*

urban sprawl becoming a problem

2 Use the timeline to answer the questions.

1 Where did urban sprawl spread in the 17th and 18th centuries?
   a London   b Paris   c Rome   d Atlanta
2 Where was urban sprawl first seen?
   a Rome   b China   c Brazil   d United States
3 What affected urban sprawl in 1918?
   a an increase in   b an increase in   c new homes were
      immigration   travel costs   built

E Critical thinking

Discuss these questions with a partner.

1 What do you think might be some advantages and disadvantages of urban sprawl?
2 How does urban sprawl affect you and where you live?
   Where I live there is / isn't a lot of urban sprawl…

Pronunciation for listening

Sounds in dates and numbers

When we talk about dates and numbers in English, it's important to get the exact date or number. Some sounds you hear may sound very similar, so you will need to practice and listen carefully to make sure you understand the information you hear.

Pay special attention to these sounds:

/i/	and	/in/	/ ɜr/	and	/ ɔr/	/i/ or /in/	and	/iz/
fifty		fifteen	thirty		forty	sixty		sixties
90–60		1916	37		47	1815		1850s

When we talk about number and date ranges, we use the word *to* to separate them.

10–20 people   *ten to twenty people*

1980–1999   *nineteen eighty to nineteen ninety-nine*

1 🎧 **4.3** Listen to the sentences from *Urban sprawl*. Circle the date you hear.

1 Others think it began in **the 1960s** / **1915** / **the 1950s**.

2 In **1980** / **1918** / **1980s**, a rapid increase in immigration after World War I resulted in greater urban growth.

3 Later, in **the 1970s** / **the 1917s** / **1917**, the sprawl continued.

2 Work with your partner. Take turns saying the numbers and dates in the box. You get one point for each date you heard correctly.

30–40   1980s   1419   50   15   1314   1980   40–90   1490s   1918

Vocabulary development

Synonyms and antonyms

Synonyms are words that have the same or very similar meanings. Antonyms are words that have opposite meanings.

	Synonym	Antonym
urban	metropolitan	rural

1 Complete the chart with the synonyms and antonyms in the box.

| ancient | busy | cheap | clean | dangerous | exciting | filthy | new |
| quiet | secure | uninteresting | unknown | valuable | well-known |

	Synonym	**Antonym**
boring		
crowded		
modern		
safe		
dirty		
expensive		
famous		

2 Read the paragraph and, only where necessary, replace the underlined words with an antonym. Use the context to help.

Berlin is the capital city of Germany. It has a population of over 3.5 million people and is ¹<u>famous</u> for its science, arts, and culture. It has 12 districts, including the ²<u>ancient</u> district of Templehof, which has many new industrial buildings, and the ³<u>crowded</u> central district of Mitte, which is often populated with a lot of tourists. There is so much to do in Berlin; some people say that Charlottenburg is a very ⁴<u>exciting</u> area of the city, but actually, it has lots of great stores! Living in Berlin is pretty ⁵<u>expensive</u>, too; in fact, houses are a lot lower in price than other European capitals.

Academic words

1 Match the words in bold with the correct definitions.

1 I want to be a doctor. They make a **considerable** amount of money.

2 The city hopes to **eventually** add new trains to the city's public transportation system.

3 The latest car model has many unique safety **features**.

4 I don't think I'm going to pass my exam because I didn't study. **Furthermore**, it was really hard.

5 **Immigration** patterns change over time.

6 My father is very sick right now. I hope he will **recover** soon.

7 They moved to the suburbs **specifically** because the schools are better there.

8 Alina and Alexander have different management **styles**.

a (adv) for one particular thing

b (n) the process in which people enter a country to live there permanently

c (n) an important part

d (n) a way that someone behaves and does things

e (adv) at the end of a process

f (adv) a connecting word that adds more information

g (v) to become fit and healthy again after illness or injury

h (adj) large in size or amount

2 Answer these questions with a partner.

1 What is your personal fashion style? What features does your wardrobe have?

2 What kind of job do you eventually hope to have?

3 Is there a considerable amount of immigration into your country, or not much?

Speaking model

You are going to learn about the simple past, clarifying, and introducing references. You are then going to use these skills to describe a past development using a timeline.

A Analyze

Look at part of a conversation during a student presentation. Choose the best words to complete the summary.

The students discuss the [1]**history / future** of Dubai. They [2]**ask questions / debate solutions** regarding the city's important moments.

A: Hello, everyone. My presentation today will be about Dubai. I will talk about the city's history, and its recent growth. Here's a copy of a timeline I'll be using. In recent years, Dubai has become very modern and metropolitan and is now one of the most important places to do business. But let's start at the beginning. The earliest date on the timeline is 1095 CE. That's the earliest recorded mention of Dubai, in a book called *The Book of Geography*. Later, …

B: Sorry. Could you say the date and the title again?

A: Yes, I said 1095 CE, and *The Book of Geography*. The next date is 1580, when a Venetian merchant talks about Dubai and its pearling industry.

C: Pearling industry? What do you mean by that?

A: In other words, people in and around Dubai went to sea to look for pearls, which they sold later.

C: Thanks.

A: Now, in the 1800s, Dubai had two problems to deal with. First was a smallpox epidemic, in 1841, and then a fire in one of its suburbs, in 1894. However, …

B: I'm sorry—what did you say?

A: Let me repeat that—epidemic in 1841, fire in 1894. But the good times were to come. Dubai was still in a good place for trade and business from around the region, and became an important port of call.

C: What do you mean by "port of call"?

A: To put it another way, it's a port that you visit when you travel by boat doing business. That was especially important in 1966, when oil was discovered below the water near Dubai. This is the next date on my timeline—in 1966 the modern-day Dubai we now know was born …

B Discuss

1 How does the speaker organize his notes about Dubai? Does he begin his presentation with old or more recent information?

2 What verb tense does he use when he's talking? Why?

3 What phrases do the students use to ask for clarification?

Grammar

Simple past: ordering past events

The simple past is used to describe events that started and finished in the past. You do not always need to mention the specific time that they happened.

I went to school (yesterday).

Dubai was famous for its pearling industry (in 1580).

Sentences with two simple past clauses can show that one thing happened and then the next thing happened, using words such as *after, once,* and *before.* This verb tense is very useful when describing a timeline.

*Dubai became famous for oil **after** the pearling industry ended.*

Sometimes you will need to give a reason why something happened. To do this, you can use a subordinate clause. The subordinate clause begins with the words *because, since,* or *as.*

*The pearling industry in Dubai died out **because** pearls were grown under controlled conditions in Japan to sell.*

If you want to introduce the result before explaining why, start your clause with the words *so (that)* or *in order to.*

*Divers in Dubai dove very deep in the sea **so (that)** they would find the most pearls.*

1 Complete the sentences with the simple past of the verbs in parentheses.

1 I _____ (research) Dubai because I'm going on holiday there.

2 Jim _____ (live) in Dubai for five years as he had a job there.

3 Oil trade _____ (be) popular after the pearling industry _____ (end).

4 Urban sprawl _____ (happen) in Babylon and China before it happened in modern day cities like London.

2 Complete the sentences.

1 I traveled to Japan _____ (**so that / since**) I could study the language.

2 I traveled to Japan last year _____ (**in order to / because**) I wanted to learn Japanese.

3 I went to school yesterday _____ (**since / so that**) I had a science test.

4 I went to school yesterday _____ (**because / in order to**) take my science test.

Asking for clarification and repetition

Speaking skill

When having academic conversations, it is sometimes difficult to follow everything that is said. There are a number of ways in English you can ask someone to explain or repeat themselves.

Asking for clarification:

What do you mean by …?

Could you give an example?

How do you spell that?

Giving clarification:

Let me explain that …

Let me put it another way …

In other words, …

Asking for repetition:

Could you repeat that?

What did you say?

Would you explain that again?

Repeating yourself:

I said …

Let me repeat that …

GLOSSARY

camel (n) a large animal with a long neck and one or two humps on its back

frosting (n) a sugary substance used to cover or fill cakes

Work with two classmates. Each classmate will read a paragraph about Dubai. As you read, your classmates will ask for clarification and repetition. Clarify or repeat as asked. Then switch roles.

The Burj al Arab is one of Dubai's most famous buildings. With 60 floors, it was the world's tallest hotel until 2009. Now it is the fourth tallest hotel in the world. The building was designed to look like the sail of a ship. It is located on an island and is connected to the mainland by a bridge. Building started in 1994. It took over five years to build. It finally opened in 1999.

The food in Dubai is wonderful. You can find food from many cultures, including Chinese, Pakistani, Lebanese, and Egyptian. In general, the food in Dubai is similar to Indian and Middle Eastern food. One of the most popular foods is carrot cake. Carrot cake has carrot pieces, nuts, and a cream-cheese frosting. Another popular food is stuffed camel, which is filled with herbs and spices.

Pronunciation for speaking

Stress in phrases connected with *and*

In short phrases connecting an adjective, noun, or verb to another using *and*, we usually stress the content words either side of *and*. The pattern looks like this: OoO.

*There are **positives and negatives** working for the automotive industry. The industry has had its **good and bad** times.*

1   Look at the sentences below. Mark the stress patterns on the phrases with *and*.

   1   The process of buying a car isn't usually quick and easy.
   2   There are positives and negatives to owning a car; it's not all good.
   3   I like peace and quiet, so electric cars are my favorite.
   4   Pinar would not tell us where she is going to college. We will have to wait and see.
   5   She's very talented; she gets top grades in arts and sciences.

2    4.4 Listen and check your answers. Then read the sentences to a partner using the correct stress pattern.

Speaking task

You will describe a timeline about your city to a partner. Your partner will take notes on your description. Then you will take notes on their timeline. You will ask for clarification and repetition.

Brainstorm

Work with a partner. Brainstorm a list of things that should be included on the timeline about your city.

_____

_____

_____

_____

Plan

Add your dates and events to your timeline.

Write sentences using the simple past that you will use as you describe your timeline to your partner.

_____

_____

_____

_____

Speak

Present your timeline to a new partner. Be prepared for him or her to ask for clarification and repetition.
Take notes on your partner's timeline.

_____

_____

_____

_____

Share

Talk with your first partner. Share something interesting you learned about your second partner's timeline.

Reflect

What do you think you would add to your timeline in 10 years?

Review

Wordlist

MACMILLAN DICTIONARY

Vocabulary preview

airbag (n)	invent (v) **	population (n) ***	seat belt (n)
ancient (adj) ***	loan (n) ***	rear (n) **	surrounding (adj) **
anti-lock brake (n)	particular (adj)***	recent (adj) ***	wheel (n) ***
forward (adv) **	passenger (n) ***	regulation (n) ***	within (prep) ***

Vocabulary development

ancient ***	dangerous ***	quiet ***	valuable ***
busy ***	exciting **	secure ***	well-known **
cheap ***	filthy *	uninteresting	
clean ***	new ***	unknown **	

Academic words

considerable (adj) ***	feature (n) ***	immigration (n) *	specifically (adv) ***
eventually (adv) ***	furthermore (adv) **	recover (v) ***	style (n) ***

Academic words review

Complete the sentences using the words in the box.

considerable   eventually   furthermore   react   specifically

1   Oliver: "What did Emma say when you told her she had failed her maths test?"
    James: "She said she wasn't surprised, so she didn't _____ too badly."
2   Gul chose to go to Stanford University _____ because it has such a good business administration program.
3   Dubai is an expensive city to live in. _____, inflation is expected to remain at around 3% this year.
4   It took Steve and Paul six hours to get to Boston because of the traffic. They _____ got there at midnight.
5   It took Jack a _____ amount of time to finish his project.

Unit review

Listening 1	☐	I can listen for dates.
Listening 2	☐	I can listen for time signals to understand when events happened.
Study skill	☐	I can manage my time effectively.
Vocabulary	☐	I can use a range of synonyms and antonyms.
Grammar	☐	I can order past events.
Speaking	☐	I can ask for clarification and repetition.

5 SUCCESS

Discussion point

Discuss with a partner.

1   Which of the things successful people do is the most important? Why?

2   Which of the things in the infographic do you already do? Do you think they will make you successful?

3   When have you enjoyed success? What did you do to celebrate?

Six things successful people do

1   **THINK POSITIVE.** If you think positively, this will change not only how you feel, but also others around you. Positive thinking is motivating, and happy people generally work faster.

2   **MAKE EFFORT.** There are no shortcuts. To develop skills to be great at anything, you have to make an effort and put in time to learn.

3   **WORK MORE.** You need to work, work, and then work some more! To be successful, you need to work long hours. Those long hours prove how much you want to succeed.

4   **AIM HIGH.** Think about your final goal and make sure you are aiming to be the best you can be. Then you can develop small steps to help you successfully reach that goal.

5   **SELL YOUR SKILL / PRODUCT.** You need to believe in your skills or product so that you can sell it to others. Knowing how to sell yourself or your product will make others want to buy!

6   **LEARN FROM YOUR MISTAKES.** Don't be afraid to make mistakes. Make sure that you learn from them so that you don't make the same mistakes twice.

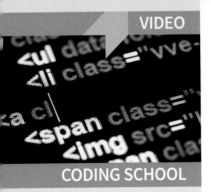

VIDEO

CODING SCHOOL

Before you watch

Answer the questions with a partner.

1   What do you think you learn at a coding school?

2   How might a coding school be different from taking a computer science course at a university?

3   What do you understand by the phrases "Silicon Valley" and "hiring partner"?

UNIT AIMS

LISTENING 1 Listening for vocabulary in context
LISTENING 2 Listening to summarize
STUDY SKILL Studying for tests

VOCABULARY Prefixes
GRAMMAR Quantifiers
SPEAKING Using discourse markers to compare and contrast

Climber on a mountain top.

While you watch

Read the sentences. Watch the video and choose *T* (True) or *F* (False).

1 Walter never studied computer coding at Wyncode Academy.　　　　　　T / F

2 The intensive computer coding course is three years long.　　　　　　T / F

3 Success is a result of merit, the effort you make, and how hard you study.　　T / F

4 Walter says learning at the coding school is faster than in traditional education.　T / F

5 The coding school is a success because it discovers the skills employers need.　T / F

After you watch

Discuss the questions with your partner.

1 Would you prefer to go to a university or a take an intensive ten-week course?

   I would prefer to go to university / take an intensive ten-week course because ...

2 Do you agree that this type of school is successful? Why / why not?

3 Walter says success is a result of the effort that you make and how hard you study. Do you think this is true?

Skill, effort or luck?

A Vocabulary preview

1 Match the words in bold with the correct definitions.

1	**admitted** (v)	a	something good that you receive because of something you have done
2	**apply** (v)	b	used to introduce a statement that makes something seem surprising
3	**effort** (n)		
4	**load** (n)	c	anything that is happening at a particular time or place
5	**reward** (n)	d	having the feeling that you get when something unexpected happens
6	**situation** (n)		
7	**surprised** (adj)	e	to say you have done something
8	**though** (conj)	f	hard work to succeed at something
		g	an amount of work that a person, piece of equipment, or system has to do at one time
		h	to make a request for a place at college or for a job

2 Complete the sentences with the correct words from Exercise 1.

1 Ali might have done better if the _____ was different and he did not have to work and go to school at the same time.

2 _____ Juan did not go to class often, he still did well on the exam.

3 Nilay was _____ she had to work so hard on her exams; she thought they would be easy.

4 Emi made an _____ to focus on her studies and spend less time going out with friends.

5 Martin studied hard and his _____ was an A on his final exam and his report card.

6 Claire _____ she did not study for the test and she failed it.

7 We need a new computer that can cope with the heavy _____.

8 Xiao is going to _____ to colleges in China and the United States.

B Before you listen

Activating prior knowledge

Read the following statements with a partner. Say whether you think they are true or false, and why.

1 *People who make a big effort and put in a lot of time studying will get good exam grades.*

2 *Some people are just very lucky and can pass an exam without studying.*

3 *Some people are just very good at taking exams because they understand the format.*

C Global listening

🎧 **5.1** Listen to *Skill, effort or luck?* and answer the questions.

1 What are the students discussing?

  a test scores   b exam grades   c English scores

2 Who wasn't completely happy with his result? Why?

  a Juan wasn't completely happy because he didn't feel he put enough effort into studying

  b Roberto wasn't completely happy because he didn't get the grades he wanted

  c Daniel wasn't completely happy because he didn't predict the right questions for the exams

D Close listening

Learning new vocabulary from context will help you focus on key information and help build your understanding of the topic. There are several strategies you can use when you hear new vocabulary:

- listen for definitions that often accompany specific vocabulary
- write vocabulary in your notes
- identify roots

Important vocabulary can be recognized in several ways. Often it:

- is stressed by speakers
- is repeated
- has pauses before and after
- is accompanied by an example
- is signaled by speakers, e.g.,

A really important concept is … A theory you should know is …

A problem we need to understand is …

1 🎧 5.2 Listen to an excerpt from the discussion and complete the paragraphs with appropriate words.

I didn't study as much as you, Roberto, but I got excellent grades. It sounds surprising, but it makes [1] _____. To be honest, I'm very good at taking exams; I work well under [2] _____ and I can predict the kind of questions they'll ask, so I only study those parts of the [3] _____. I really enjoyed the exams I took, actually!

Wow, that's an amazing [4] _____ to have, Daniel. Honestly, I feel really [5] _____. I worked really hard in all of my classes because I needed to do well so that I could apply for [6] _____ to college. My goal is to get into medical school one day, so I need good grades. All of my studying paid off!

2 Compare your paragraphs with a partner.

E Critical thinking

Discuss these questions in a group.

1 Which of the students in *Skill, effort or luck?* is most deserving of a reward? Why?
   I think … deserves to be rewarded because …

2 Do you think the students got what they deserved? Why / why not?
   I think … got what he deserved because …

3 Which student are you most like? How are you similar? How are you different?
   I am most like … We both …

Studying for tests

1 Discuss these questions with a partner.

1 Do you think it is easy or hard to study for tests? Why?

2 How do you feel when you learn you are going to have an important test?

3 What materials do you study before a test? For example, your lecture notes, textbooks, online materials, or other students' notes?

2 Look at these tips for studying for tests. Discuss each one with a partner. Which ones are the most important?

1 Schedule your time wisely. Think about how much material you have to study. Plan to start studying several days or a week before. Do not wait until the night before the test.

2 Go to review sessions.

3 Ask the instructor what chapters or content will be on the test. Schedule an appointment or ask the instructor in class. They can often help you focus on certain materials.

4 Eat well beforehand so you don't get distracted by hunger during the test.

5 Go to sleep early, and don't stay up all night trying to "cram." If you are tired, you won't focus on the test. Don't forget to set an alarm so you won't miss the test.

6 Make study guides from the textbook and lecture notes. This will save you time later. You won't have to reread chapters or remember what your notes mean if you create guides each week.

7 Arrive early to find a good seat where you won't be distracted.

8 Find a quiet place and study there consistently. Look for a place that is quiet and private. Study in the same place and at the same time each day.

3 Discuss these questions with a partner.

1 Which of these tips do you already do? Which will you start to use in the future?

2 Do you have a place to study? Where is it? Why is it good for studying?

3 What other tips do you think should be added to the list?

What is success?

A Vocabulary preview

1 Complete the text with words in the box. There is one which is not used.

> according to   attempted   career   disagree
> graduate   minimum   society   wage

¹ _____ some people, you need to ² _____ from college to have a successful ³ _____ in business. They think that if you do not go to college, then you will get a job that pays only ⁴ _____ wage. Other people ⁵ _____ with this idea. To support their point, they use Bill Gates and Steve Jobs as examples. Both Gates and Jobs were successful, but neither of them graduated from college. They both ⁶ _____ to start companies even without having a business degree. Their companies were successful. In fact, because ⁷ _____ has placed such importance on technology, their companies are two of the most successful in the world.

2 Answer the questions with a partner.

1 According to your parents, what are the most important subjects to study? Do you agree or disagree?

2 Have you ever attempted something several times before succeeding?

B Before you listen

Activating prior knowledge

1 Look at the list of achievements. Check (✓) the things you have already achieved. Put a question mark (?) by the things you plan to achieve later.

getting a college degree

getting married

winning a sports game

completing a school project

being accepted to college

raising a family

2 Look at the quote below and the list of achievements in Question 1. Then answer the questions.

> *A doctor is just as successful as a maid if they're both doing what they planned to do.*

1 What is the speaker talking about?

2 What do you think will be his answer to the question, "What is success?"

C Global listening

Speakers will often summarize their ideas at the end or near the end of their talk. It's useful to make a note of their summaries because they will contain:

- main ideas
- the most important supporting details
- a credit to the source.

They don't contain facts, statistics, details, examples, or opinion.

Listening to summarize

1 🎧 5.3 Listen to *What is success?* Circle the best short summary.

   a   Success is about achieving your goals.

   b   Success is about doing what you planned to do.

2 Look at these notes. Check (✓) the ideas that should be included in a summary of the presentation.

   1 ☐ examples of success are money, work, and college

   2 ☐ success is the achievement of something you planned or attempted

   3 ☐ the key is that YOU plan

   4 ☐ running a marathon is a good example

   5 ☐ success is determined by the individual

   6 ☐ doctors and maids are both successful

   7 ☐ the specifics are different for everyone

   8 ☐ working hard, practicing, and focusing are important to success

   9 ☐ the speaker believes rich men and poor men can both be successful

3 Choose the best summary, A or B. Give reasons for your choice.

A Success is achieving something you planned or attempted, such as making a lot of money or going to college. The key is planning what you want and then trying to do it. Success is determined by each person and not by others. Most people feel that graduating from college makes you successful, but men like Bill Gates didn't graduate, and they are still considered successful. It doesn't matter if a person is a doctor or a maid. Both can be successful because the specifics are different for each person. There are many characteristics of successful people. For example, successful people work hard and focus. In general, rich people and poor people can be successful if they work hard.

B Success is achieving something you planned or attempted. The key is to plan what you want and then try to do it. Success is determined by the individual and not by what others want. Therefore, everyone's idea of success is different. The characteristics for achieving success are similar, but the end goal is different. In general, if you choose it, plan it, and then attempt it, then you are successful.

Listening for details

D Close listening

🎧 **5.3** Listen to *What is success?* again. Write *T* (True) or *F* (False).

1 Success is always dictated by society. ____

2 You don't have to finish college to be successful. ____

3 Bill Gates never intended to start a company. ____

4 The speaker believes that doctors are more successful than maids. ____

5 Earning money isn't a sign of success. ____

6 Everybody agrees on what success is. ____

E Critical thinking

Discuss these questions in a group.

1 Do you agree that people in all kinds of jobs are equally successful if they are doing what they planned to do? Why / why not?

2 Do you think success is determined by doing one thing well, like winning a marathon, or by doing a lot of things?

3 Do you think it is possible to be more successful than another person? Why / why not?

Pronunciation for listening

Homophones

Homophones are words that have the same pronunciation, and sometimes the same spelling, but with different meanings. For example, *compliment* and *complement*.

You can usually determine which word is being used by the words that come before and after it.

Those **complement** *my background.*

I'll **compliment** *you on your hard work.*

1 🎧 5.4 Listen to the sentences and choose the correct homophone.

   1 a blue
      b blew
   2 a night
      b knight
   3 a do
      b due
   4 a seams
      b seems
   5 a weather
      b whether

2 Make five new sentences using one of the homophones from Exercise 1 on each line.

blue / blew   night / knight   do / due   seams / seems   weather / whether

   1 *The assignment was due at the end of February.*
   2 _____
   3 _____
   4 _____
   5 _____

3 Read your sentences from Exercise 2 to a partner and see if they can figure out the correct homophone.

Vocabulary development

Prefixes

A prefix is a short letter group added to the beginning of a word that changes its meaning. Knowing what the prefix means can help you determine the meaning of a word.

Some common prefixes in English are:

Prefix	Meaning	Example
dis-	opposite	disagree
in-	not	inconvenient
im-	not	impossible
re-	again	return
over-	too / more	overachiever

1 Complete the chart with prefixes in the box.

Prefix / Word	Meaning
¹____appear	go away
²____consistent	not the same
dislike	³_____
incomplete	⁴_____
⁵____patient	not wanting to wait
rewrite	⁶_____
overcautious	⁷_____
⁸____arrange	put into a different order

2 Complete the questions with a word from Exercise 1. One word isn't used.

1 Is there anything you wish would _____ to make your life easier?

2 What kind of food do you _____ most?

3 Have you ever turned in an _____ homework assignment?

4 Is it OK to be late or do you get _____ when you have to wait for someone?

5 Have you ever had to _____ an appointment because you didn't have time to go?

6 Has a teacher ever asked you to _____ a paper?

7 Is there a class in which your grades are _____, sometimes they are high and sometimes they are low? Why is this?

3 Work with a partner. Ask and answer the questions from Exercise 2.

Academic words

1 Match the words in bold with the correct definitions.

1 The **author** spent four years writing his latest book.

2 The students were **tense** about their exam results.

3 Jim didn't want his bad test results to **affect** his overall grade.

4 I like my science professor because she **defines** important words.

5 I did not have much time to study, but I still got an **adequate** grade on the final exam.

6 The pictures in the science book **illustrate** the difficult concepts.

7 Michael didn't **invest** much time practicing so he wasn't surprised he failed his driver's test.

8 The coffee was a perfect **complement** to the dessert we ordered.

a _____ (v) put money, time, or effort into something

b _____ (v) have an effect on

c _____ (adj) acceptable

d _____ (v) states the meaning of

e _____ (adj) feeling nervous and not relaxed, usually because you are worried about what is going to happen

f _____ (v) something added to make it easier or better

g _____ (n) someone who writes books as their job

h _____ (v) provide a visual explanation

2 Answer the questions with a partner.

1 If you are stressed, does it affect how well you perform in tests?

2 What is the latest thing you read about or saw in the news? How did it affect people?

3 What made you tense recently? Why?

4 What is the best thing you have ever read? Who was the author?

Speaking model

You are going to learn about quantifiers, discourse markers to compare and contrast, and pronunciation of discourse markers. You are then going to use these skills to give a presentation that compares and contrasts data.

A Model

What role do these factors play in getting a job?

Fig. 1

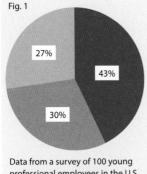

Data from a survey of 100 young professional employees in the U.S.

Fig. 2

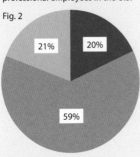

Data from a survey of 100 young professional employees in the U.K.

 education

 work experience

luck

I would like to present the results of Michigan's New University's research study on what role education and previous work experience play in getting a job. Which is more important? The data presented illustrate a significant contrast in what young professionals in the U.S. believe is the most important factor in getting a job, compared to what young professionals in the U.K. believe is the most important factor in getting a job. Two hundred young professionals were surveyed in the U.S. and the U.K. in 2017 and below you can see the findings. According to the pie chart here, 43% of survey respondents said exam results are the most important factor in getting a job in the U.S. The percentage of people that said exam results were the most important factor in getting a job in the U.K. was significantly lower, at 20%. You can see an inconsistent opinion in the role people from both countries think previous work experience plays, too. In the U.S., only 30% of the respondents said previous work experience was very important in getting a job. In contrast, a huge 59% of those surveyed thought the same in the U.K. The rest of the respondents in both countries, so that is 27% in the U.S. and only 21% in the UK, said that neither experience nor education played a part in getting a job— it's all down to luck! In conclusion, more people surveyed in the U.K. seem to believe getting a job is based on prior work experience, whereas more people in the U.S. think exams are most important.

Work with a partner. Read the model and answer the questions below.

1 How does the speaker begin their presentation? Is this a good start?

2 Do you think the speaker presented the information in a logical order?

3 What words does the speaker use to compare and contrast the data?

B Discuss

1 Do you think exams are more or less important than previous work experience when applying for a new job? Why?

2 Do you think luck has any influence on whether you get a job?

3 What job would you like to have when you finish studying?

Grammar

Quantifiers

Quantifiers are used to give more information about the number of something, such as how much or how many of something there is.

Two of the most common are:

a few of   *a lot of*

These quantifiers indicate either more or less of something:

more: a lot of, significantly, considerably, most

less: a little, slightly, marginally, least

*There are **considerably** more respondents who feel …*

*There was only a **marginal** difference between …*

1   Complete the sentences using the correct quantifier.

1   Marta did **significantly** / **slightly** better on the second math test; she improved from a D to an A.

2   Ji Hye did not use the **most** / **least** sources. She had three sources for her paper, but the other students included five.

3   **A lot of** / **A few** fans waited to see the soccer team at the airport even though they had lost the game.

4   There was only a **considerable** / **marginal** difference between the figures. I was surprised that it was such a small number.

5   David sent **slightly** / **considerably** longer email messages than his brother; his were over two paragraphs longer than his brother's.

6   What idea do you think the **most** / **least** people will like? That is the one we should choose.

2   Read the sentences and write a quantifier before the word in bold. More than one answer is possible.

1   _____ **respondents** felt that computer skills were important in the workplace.

2   Yoohee thinks that workers should make _____ **effort** if they want to succeed.

3   The chart shows that employees think that having a college degree is only _____ **necessary**.

4   Last year, college dropouts were getting only _____ **criticism** from the media. Now they are getting more.

5   Society thinks that certain types of jobs deserve _____ **more respect** than others.

6   If you only put in _____ **effort**, you might not get the best grades.

Speaking skill

When giving a presentation that includes data or facts, you may have to compare and contrast the information. To compare information means to look for the similarities, whereas to contrast information means to highlight the differences. Some common language used to compare and contrast is:

as … as	*likewise*
conversely	*on the contrary*
in contrast	*similarly*
in the same way	*the same as*
like	*unlike*

*The library at Cambridge is **as** good **as** the library at Oxford.*

*I like studying math. **Similarly**, I enjoy learning about science, too.*

*I like reading articles in sociology journals. **Conversely**, articles in medical journals are not my favorite reading material.*

1 Organize the phrases used to compare and contrast into the correct category.

Compare	Contrast

2 Choose the best word to complete each sentence.

1 Most people feel effort is related to success. **However** / **Similarly**, only a few people believe that luck is related to success.

2 You can see from the data that 20% believe that skill plays a role. **Similarly** / **In contrast**, over 70% believe that effort plays a role.

3 Both surveys had **the same** / **a different** number of respondents with 200.

4 The salesmen needed to meet their sales goals this month. This is **similar to** / **unlike** warehouse workers who do not have to make any sales.

5 I successfully learned how to play the piano; **however** / **similarly**, I was never able to learn how to play the violin.

6 The company was very successful with their marketing of the new product. **Similarly** / **Conversely**, marketing of the older products were not as profitable.

Pronunciation for speaking

Stress in modifiers before data

When comparing and contrasting data, we often use modifiers before figures or information to emphasize that the data is surprising or unexpected. These modifiers are normally stressed to show that the number that follows them is a surprise.

*In contrast, a **huge** 69% of those surveyed thought …*

*… so that is 27% in the U.S. and **only** 21% in the U.K. …*

*An **impressive** 79% of students responded …*

*A **remarkable** number of students said they didn't think work experience was important …*

*As **many as** / **much as** 250 people agreed that …*

1 🎧 5.5 Listen and complete the sentences with the correct modifier.

1 There was a _____ difference in the number of students that enrolled in the class in 2017 compared to 2018.

2 The data showed a _____ number of students feel pressured to do well in exams.

3 _____ 3% of interviewees said that they would like to do sports in their free time.

4 _____ 90% of respondents agreed that they would like the university to open a new science block.

5 A _____ 98% of interviewees felt skill was very important in exam performance.

6 An _____ 56% of respondents actually said they would like to take a different course next year.

2 Practice saying the sentences in Exercise 1 with a partner. Stress the modifiers.

Speaking task

Use data to present a small talk on the most important factor that influences exam pass rates.

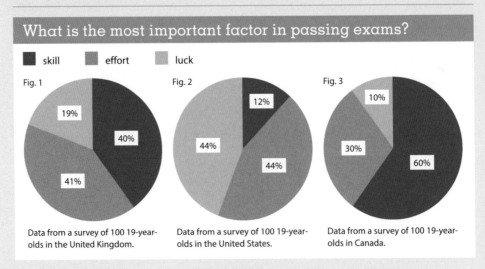

What is the most important factor in passing exams?

■ skill ■ effort ■ luck

Fig. 1
19% 40% 41%

Fig. 2
12% 44% 44%

Fig. 3
10% 30% 60%

Data from a survey of 100 19-year-olds in the United Kingdom.

Data from a survey of 100 19-year-olds in the United States.

Data from a survey of 100 19-year-olds in the Canada.

Brainstorm

Work in a small group. Talk about whether each piece of data in the charts should be compared or contrasted. Are they the same or different? Make a list of words you can use in your presentation.

Plan

1 Decide on the structure of your presentation. What is the most important piece of data? Should that be presented first or last?

2 What discourse markers are you going to use to compare the information? What quantifiers?

3 What do you think the results show? How can you summarize the data?

Speak

Present your presentation to a small group.

Share

Talk to your group. Whose presentation was the most effective and why?

Reflect

Think about your presentations. Did you organize the data effectively? Did you use discourse markers and quantifiers? What could you have done differently?

Review

Wordlist

MACMILLAN
DICTIONARY

Vocabulary preview

according to (prep) ***	effort (n) ***	society (n) ***
admit (v) ***	graduate (v) **	surprised (adj) ***
apply (v) ***	load (n) ***	though (conj) ***
attempted (adj) ***	minimum (adj) **	wage (n) ***
career (n) ***	reward (n) **	
disagree (v) **	situation (n) ***	

Vocabulary development

disappear (v) ***	impatient (adj) *	inconsistent (adj)	rearrange (v)
dislike (v) **	incomplete (adj)	overcautious (adj)	rewrite (v) *

Academic words

adequate (adj) ***	complement (v) *	invest (v) ***
affect (v) ***	define (v) ***	tense (adj) *
author (n) ***	illustrate (v) ***	

Academic words review

Complete the sentences using the words in the box.

author	define	illustrate	immigration	invest

1 When writing an essay, it is a good idea to use examples to _____ what you are trying to say.

2 I love detective novels and Sue Grafton is my favorite _____.

3 There are so many different savings plans available that it is difficult to decide how to _____ your money.

4 When writing a job description, it is important to _____ the responsibilities of the role.

5 The movement of people coming to live in another country is called _____.

Unit review

Listening 1	☐	I can listen to understand key vocabulary in context.
Listening 2	☐	I can listen and then summarize what I have heard.
Study skill	☐	I can study effectively for tests.
Vocabulary	☐	I can use a range of prefixes to change the meanings of words.
Grammar	☐	I can use a range of quantifiers to say how many or much there is.
Speaking	☐	I can use a range of words and phrases to compare and contrast information.

UNDER PRESSURE

We all have stress. Whether it's caused by money worries, tomorrow's exam, or pressure at work, its effects can be harmful. But there are ways to manage our stress.

BREATHE DEEPLY
Try breathing in through your nose and out through your mouth.

EXERCISE
What's good for your overall health also keeps stress levels low.

LISTEN TO MUSIC
Studies show that listening to your favorite music lowers your stress.

GET A PET
If you're stressed and don't have a pet, consider a trip to the pet store.

PLAN AHEAD
A simple, "If X happens, I'll do Y," exercise can help you face new challenges.

STAY POSITIVE
Keep a list of positives in your mind to go to when you start to feel stressed.

Discussion point

Discuss with a partner.

1 Which idea do you think is the most / least helpful for managing stress?

   I think the most / least helpful idea is to …

2 What are some things that can cause stress or pressure?

   Exams / Traffic / Speaking in front of others can cause a lot of stress.

3 Which tips can help reduce the stress for things you mentioned? What are some other ways to manage stress or pressure?

   I think it's helpful to …

VIDEO

FLOWER-ARRANGING BUSINESSMEN

Before you watch

Predict which numbers complete each sentence. One number is not used.

1   20   500   15 million

1 The number of people who do flower arranging is about _____ million.
2 62-year-old Minoru started flower-arranging evening classes _____ years ago.
3 The tradition of flower arranging started _____ years ago.

UNIT AIMS

LISTENING 1 Listening for how opinions are supported
LISTENING 2 Listening for cause and effect
STUDY SKILLS Enabling good discussion

VOCABULARY Collocations: Expressions with *get*
GRAMMAR Giving advice using modals in conditional sentences
SPEAKING Explaining something you don't know the word for

A nut being cracked.

While you watch

1 Watch the video and check your answers to the *Before you watch*.

2 Read the summary and check that you understand the vocabulary. Choose the correct answer.

The video is based in ¹ **Tokyo / Kuala Lumpur**. It first shows a man ² **choosing flowers in a shop / putting flowers in a vase**. The school in the video has more ³ **men / women**. People say they do flower arranging because ⁴ **it is less painful than sports / it relaxes them**.

After you watch

Answer the questions with a partner.

1 Would you like to try flower arranging to manage stress and feel calm? Why / why not?

Yes, I think it would be a good idea because …

No, I don't like that idea very much because …

2 Which do you prefer: creative hobbies or sports? Why?

3 Why do you think the men in this video get stressed? Will people with different jobs have different reasons?

Peer pressure

A Vocabulary preview

1 Match the words in bold with the correct definitions.

1	**call sb sth** (phr v)	a	to have not included someone or something
2	**direct** (adj)	b	to say what you think in a clear and honest way
3	**exact** (adj)	c	referring to one particular thing and no other
4	**left out** (phr v)	d	to help someone when they are having a difficult time
5	**logical** (adj)	e	connecting ideas or reasons in a sensible way
6	**peer** (n)	f	to behave in a sensible and fair way
7	**reasonable** (adj)	g	someone who is the same age as another person
8	**support** (v)	h	to use a particular name or title for someone

2 Complete the sentences with the correct word from Exercise 1.

1 Good friends will always _____ you, even during bad times.

2 It's _____ to expect friends to be there for you if you have a problem.

3 If you don't like something your friend is doing, be _____ and just tell them.

4 The best person to get advice from is a _____, not a parent or teacher.

5 If you think of the situation in a _____ way, you'll see it's not really a big problem.

6 People should never get angry if a friend doesn't show up at the _____ time.

7 My friends used to _____ Logical Lisa because I was always solving problems!

8 Last week my friends all went to the park and didn't invite me. I felt _____.

3 Work with a partner. Look at sentences 1–6. Which do you agree with? Give your opinion. Now look at sentences 7–8. Have you ever been in a similar situation? Describe it.

B Before you listen

Read the definition of peer pressure. Then read the situations below. Which are examples of peer pressure? Why?

1 Terry's friends try to get him to stay out after 9:00, even though they know he has to be home before then.

2 Hamid's parents are pressuring him to study medicine like his sister, but he wants to study engineering.

3 Joel likes to buy the shoes that he sees his favorite soccer star wearing on TV.

4 Megan's classmates laugh and point at her cell phone because it's an older model.

5 Three of Hasna's classmates are part of a study group that always does well on tests. They keep encouraging her to join their group.

peer pressure /ˈpɪər ˌpreʃər/
NOUN [U]
the effect that people your own age have on the way you act, in order to get you to behave the way they do

C Global listening

🎧 6.1 Listen to *Peer pressure*. Number the topics from 1 to 6 in the order Laila and Susan discuss them. There is one topic they do not discuss.

a ___ two types of peer pressure

b ___ the definition of peer pressure

c ___ if peer pressure can be positive

d ___ why people pressure others

e ___ how to avoid peer pressure

f ___ when most peer pressure situations occur

g ___ who to talk to if you feel peer pressure

GLOSSARY

indirect (adj) not communicated in a direct way

D Close listening

1 🎧 **6.1** Listen to *Peer pressure* again. Who gives these opinions? Write *L* (Laila) or *S* (Susan).

1 Peer pressure is the pressure you get from your friends. ___
2 Most peer pressure situations occur during school. ___
3 It's easy to be logical with people. ___
4 The best way to avoid peer pressure is to make friends with people who behave like you. ___
5 Peer pressure can be a positive thing. ___

Listening for how opinions are supported

It is important to understand how opinions are supported in a talk or discussion. An opinion that is not supported may not be a convincing one. Phrases that signal supporting opinions include:

Giving an example: *For example, … / For instance, …*

Explaining further: *Let me explain … / Let me just add that …*

Giving a reason: *This is because … / The reason for this is …*

2 🎧 **6.2** Listen to these excerpts. Match to complete them.

1 For example,
2 This is because
3 Let me just add that
4 The reason for this is
5 Let me explain.

a at school you're with your peers all day.
b If my friends get good grades, I'll try and do the same.
c I have some experience with people like that.
d my friends sometimes try and get me to do things I shouldn't.
e you'll be less likely to get in trouble.

E Critical thinking

Discuss these questions in a group.

1 Is peer pressure a big problem in your college?
2 What are some other examples of positive peer pressure? Have you experienced any of them?

… is an example of positive peer pressure. For instance, I once …

Pronunciation for listening

Taking time to think

Speakers often take time to think about what they are going to say next. They may speak more slowly or pause while they think. They may also use phrases such as *Let's see …*, *Let me think …*, and *you know*, as well as fillers like *um …*, *uh …*, *well …* and *OK*.

1 🎧 **6.3** Listen to six sentences. Does the speaker take time to think? Check (✓) the correct box.

	Takes time to think	Doesn't take time to think
1	☐	☐
2	☐	☐
3	☐	☐
4	☐	☐
5	☐	☐
6	☐	☐

2 🎧 **6.4** Listen to these sentences from *Peer pressure*. Write a / where the speakers take time to think. The first one has been done for you.

1   Let's see. / I think peer pressure / is the pressure you get from your friends.
2   Um, I think most peer pressure situations occur at school.
3   I think it's after school.
4   So, which is worse?
5   Um, I suppose a teacher.
6   In my opinion, no.

3 🎧 **6.5** Listen to the excerpt from *Peer pressure*. Complete the blanks with the fillers and phrases you hear.

Susan: It's just terrible when your peers don't include you. Don't you agree?

Laila: [1] _____, _____ … No, I don't think direct pressure is so bad. Pressure that is not direct seems worse.

Susan: Why is that?

Laila: [2] _____, I think it's easier to deal with direct pressure and be … [3] _____ … I can't think of the exact word. It's … [4] _____ … similar to *reasonable*.

Exam pressure

A Vocabulary preview

1 Match the words in bold with the correct definitions below.

   a   I sometimes **compete** with my friends to see who can get the best grades.

   b   I have many **demands** on my time because I study, work, and play sports.

   c   I try to get good grades so I don't **disappoint** the people in my family.

   d   When things **distract** me during an exam, I get very annoyed.

   e   My family has high **expectations** of me doing well on my exams.

   f   I usually **outline** the ideas of my essay for my professor to check.

   g   I don't believe that caffeine has a **psychological** effect on your brain.

   h   I try hard to **reduce** the amount of stress in my life.

   1   _____ (v) to make someone unhappy because you didn't do something, or do it well

   2   _____ (v) to make something smaller or less in size

   3   _____ (v) to try to be more successful than someone else

   4   _____ (n) involving or affecting your mind

   5   _____ (v) to give the main ideas of a plan or a piece of writing without all the details

   6   _____ (n) the belief that something will happen

   7   _____ (v) to get someone's attention and stop them from concentrating

   8   _____ (n) things that need to be done in a particular situation

2 Which of the sentences from Exercise 1 are true for you? Tell a partner.

B Before you listen

Activating prior knowledge

1 How stressed do you get when you take an exam? Put an X on the line.

←——————————————————————————————————→

Extremely stressed   Very stressed   A little stressed   Not stressed at all

2 Work in a group. Compare your ideas and discuss these questions.

   1   Who gets the most stressed? The least stressed?

   2   How do you feel before an exam? During an exam? After an exam?

   3   What do you think causes your stress?

C Global listening

🎧 **6.6** Listen to the lecture. Check (✓) the topics the professor talks about.

1 ☐ statistics about exam pressure
2 ☐ her personal experience with exam pressure
3 ☐ causes of exam pressure
4 ☐ results of a recent experiment
5 ☐ effects of exam pressure
6 ☐ ways to deal with exam pressure
7 ☐ why teachers should not give students tests

Listening for main ideas

GLOSSARY

fit in (phr v) to be accepted by a group of people because you are similar to them

self-esteem (n) the feeling that you are as important as other people and that you deserve to be treated well

Listening for cause
and effect

D Close listening

A cause is an event or action that makes something else happen. As effect is a direct result of that action. In these examples, the connecting words and phrases that signal cause-and-effect relationships are in bold. The cause is underlined once, and its effect is underlined twice.

Exam pressure **caused** / **resulted in** / **was the reason for** their parent's disappointment.

A person may feel pressure during an exam. **As a result, / Consequently,** this person may get sick.

Students may develop poor eating habits **because of** / **as a result of** exam pressure.

Her lack of motivation **was due to** / **was caused by** the pressures of exams.

1 6.7 Listen to an excerpt from the lecture. Number the causes of exam pressure from 1 to 7 in the order they are mentioned.

☐ the test itself

☐ being unprepared

☐ the room and test-taking environment

☐ when the test is scheduled

☐ competition from peers

☐ high expectations from parents

☐ other people in the exam room

2 6.8 Listen to another excerpt from the lecture. Complete the summary with words and phrases from the box.

anxious   as a result of   depression   disappointment
may result in   physical   serious

Many students feel [1] _____ during a test because of exam pressure, but it's usually not so [2]_____. Others may not feel well during an exam [3] _____ the pressure. They may feel sick, not sleep well, or have difficulty breathing. Not all effects are [4]_____. Students may get angry, feel lost, or even develop [5]_____. All this [6]_____ low self-esteem, a lack of motivation, or [7]_____ from parents.

E Critical thinking

Discuss these questions in a group.

1 How is exam stress similar to peer pressure?

2 Do you agree with the causes and effects mentioned in the lecture? Can you add any more?

Study skills   Enabling good discussion

Include everyone

Speak to everyone in the group, not just individuals. Make sure that everyone has a chance to speak.

Listen to other students

Your fellow students deserve your respectful attention - just as you deserve theirs.

Build on other people's ideas

That's an important point you made, for several reasons ...

If you agree

Express your agreement: *So do I ... , Yes, that's true ...*

If you disagree

Express your disagreement: Instead of just rejecting other people's ideas, explore them: *What makes you think that?*

Offer information

Share your knowledge: *There's some useful information on that in ...*

© Stella Cottrell (2013)

1   These things were said during a discussion. Match them to the tips.

1   "Let me just quickly write that down."

2   "I agree with your point, and I'd like to add ..."

3   "I like what you just said. I've never thought about that before."

4   "That's similar to what I learned last year in my psychology class."

5   "Let's move in a circle so we can see each other. Can everyone hear me?"

6   "I don't know what you mean exactly. Can you say it another way?"

a   Check that everyone can see and hear everyone else.

b   Be open to hearing something new.

c   Note down useful information.

d   If you don't understand something, ask.

e   Link what you hear to what you already know.

f   Make contributions—for example, raise points that interest you.

2   Work in a group. Discuss the following question. Use the tips from Exercise 1 to guide your discussion.

How many exams should a typical class have per year?

Vocabulary development

Collocations with *get*

Many words and phrases can follow *get*. Look at these examples.

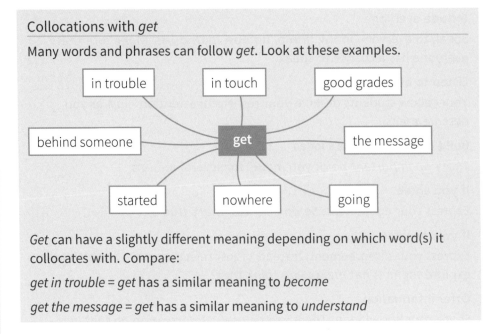

Get can have a slightly different meaning depending on which word(s) it collocates with. Compare:

get in trouble = *get* has a similar meaning to *become*

get the message = *get* has a similar meaning to *understand*

1 Complete the sentences with a collocation with *get*.

1 When you begin something, you get _____ doing it.

2 You get _____ when you completely fail to achieve something.

3 You get _____ when you understand what is said or meant.

4 To get _____ means to get a high score in the subjects you study.

5 When someone wants you to get _____, they want you to contact them.

6 Another way to say you support someone is to say you get _____.

7 When you say you need to get _____ it means you need to leave.

8 If you get _____ it means you probably did something bad.

2 Replace the crossed out words with a collocation with *get*.

 get in touch
1 Feel free to ~~contact me~~ if you want to study together.

2 We have to finish this project today so let's ~~begin~~.

3 Sam studied very hard for his exam as he didn't want to ~~be punished~~.

4 You don't have to tell me again. I ~~understand what you mean~~.

5 It's a good idea to try to ~~do well~~ on your exams.

6 If you choose to make a complaint about the hotel, you know I will ~~support you~~.

7 We need to ~~start our trip~~ if we want to arrive by the evening.

8 When I try to study for tests I feel like I ~~don't progress~~. I never seem to improve.

Academic words

1 Match the words in bold with the correct definitions.

1 **depression** (n)   a to happen, especially unexpectedly

2 **factor** (n)   b relating to only one thing or type of thing

3 **instance** (n)   c a person's gender; being male or female

4 **occur** (v)   d the study of the mind and how it affects behavior

5 **psychology** (n)   e an example of something happening

6 **revise** (v)   f something that affects if or how an event happens

7 **sex** (n)   g a feeling of being extremely unhappy

8 **specific** (adj)   h to change, improve, or make additions to something

2 Complete the opinions with the words from Exercise 1.

1 I think that performing badly on an exam can lead to _____ in some students.

2 If a student finds a(n) _____ of a teacher making a mistake while correcting an exam, they shouldn't say anything.

3 Every student should take a(n) _____ class to better understand how to deal with stress.

4 Students that think they don't need to study should _____ their opinion.

5 If cheating and other bad behavior _____ during an exam, the best thing to do is tell a teacher.

6 To me, magazines and websites that give general advice on how to deal with stress are not helpful. They need to give more _____ advice for it to be helpful.

7 In my opinion, the main _____ that can affect a student's self-esteem is getting poor grades.

8 It doesn't matter what _____ a student is—professors should treat males and females exactly the same way in class.

3 Which opinion from Exercise 2 do you agree with the most? Tell a partner. Be sure you support your opinion.

Speaking model

You are going to learn about giving advice using conditional sentences, pronouncing consonant sounds at word boundaries, and language explaining something you don't know the word for. You are then going to use these skills to discuss ways to reduce pressure for students.

A Analyze

1 Three students are discussing when pressure is a bad thing. Read the model. Add the sentences to the correct places.

> a My parents expect a lot from me.   b I don't have a lot of time to prepare for exams.
> c I stay home all the time.   d I know I eat too much junk food.

Yuki: OK, let's get started. Do you think pressure is always a bad thing?

Omar: I think it is. I'm under a lot of pressure, and it has a negative effect on me. For example, [1]___ I have a pretty bad diet. And I don't get much physical exercise.

Sara: What causes the pressure you face?

Omar: [2]___ I don't want to disappoint them, so I really try to get good grades. I really don't want to get in trouble! What about you?

Yuki: I'm under pressure, too. [3]___ As a result, I don't get good grades.

Omar: Maybe you could take fewer classes.

Yuki: Yeah, that's a good idea. I might do that next semester.

Sara: I have pressure, too, but it's more financial than academic. I feel like I never have enough money. So what do I do? [4]___

Omar: Have you thought about getting a job?

2 List the causes and effects of pressure from the model.

	Causes of pressure	Effects of pressure
Omar		
Yuki		
Sara		

B Discuss

Answer the questions with a partner.

1 What kind of pressure does each student have? Who do you think is under the most pressure?

... 's pressure is financial / academic / personal.

2 What advice would you give each speaker?

I would tell / encourage ... to ...

Grammar

Giving advice using modals in conditional sentences

We can use the present real conditional to give advice. Use a modal in the main clause.

if + simple present, modal + base verb	*If you **feel** stressed out, you **might try** and **relax**.*
	*If you **feel** pressure from peers, you **should get** help.*
	*If nothing **works**, you **could try** talking to another person.*

We can also use the present unreal conditional to give advice. Here you are imagining what you would do if the condition were to happen.

| if + simple past, *would* + base verb | *If I **were** you, I **would see** what works best for you.* |

Note: after the *if* clause, we always use a comma.

1 Unscramble and rewrite the present real conditional sentences. Add commas and periods as necessary.

1 If / you / you / should ask the teacher / don't understand the directions

_____

2 If / you / you / feel anxious during an exam / might try breathing deeply

_____

3 If / you / you / should answer the easy questions / don't have enough time

_____

4 If / you / you / could ask to take it later / miss the exam

_____

5 If / you / you / are well-prepared / shouldn't have any problems

_____

6 If / you / you / don't have good test-taking skills / might consider taking a class

_____

2 Write advice to these people. Begin with *If I were you, …*

1 A: I sometimes feel sick during an exam.
B: _____.

2 A: I never have enough time to finish an exam.
B: _____.

3 A: I don't think this exam question is fair.
B: _____.

Speaking skill

We sometimes don't know the exact word for something. When we speak, it's not always practical to use a dictionary, so we need to make ourselves understood in other ways. We can say what the word is similar to, what kind of thing it is, or give the meaning of the word.

Saying you don't know a word	Explaining the word
I can't think of the exact word.	*It's similar to reasonable.*
I'm not sure how you say it in English.	*It's a kind of pressure you get from friends.*
What's the word I'm thinking of?	*It's a person who gives professional advice.*

1 Match the sentences with the word or phrase it describes.

1 It means to stay away from someone or something.   a exercise

2 It's another word for *test*.   b get started

3 It's the opposite of *increase*.   c avoid

4 It's an expression that's similar to *be very surprised*.   d get a shock

5 It means the same as *begin*.   e reduce

6 It's something you can do to manage your stress.   f exam

2 Complete the conversations with words and expressions from the unit.

1 A: I'm not sure how to say this in English. It's similar to *worried* or *nervous*.

   B: Is it _____?

2 A: I don't know the exact word. It means someone who is the same age as another person.

   B: Do you mean _____?

3 A: I can't think of the exact expression. It means *to contact someone*.

   B: You must mean *to get* _____.

4 A: I forgot the exact word. It's the kind of pressure that is clear and honest.

   B: Oh, I think you mean _____ pressure.

5 A: How do I say this? It's a two-word expression that means *to leave*.

   B: Is it *to* _____?

6 A: What's the word I'm thinking of? It's the verb form of *competition*.

   B: It's _____.

3 Work in groups. Take turns explaining these words. Choose words you know or use a dictionary to help you.

cause   effect   motivation   opinion   positive   self-esteem   stress

This is the opposite of …   *It's similar to …*   *Is it …?*

Pronunciation for speaking

Consonant sounds at word boundaries

In connected speech, it's often hard to hear where one word ends and the other begins. When a word ends with a consonant and the next word begins with a vowel, it often sounds like the consonant is at the beginning of the next word. This is a type of catenation.

there's another idea

how about a coffee?

put on a dress

they own the store

When a word ends with a consonant and the next word begins with a similar consonant sound, speakers will usually miss one of the sounds out to make the sentence easier to say. This is called elision.

you must tell him

the wind blows east

he put down the tools

we worked together

1 🎧 6.9 Listen to the conversation. Circle where the consonant sound moves to the beginning of the next word.

Shira: Anna, we can't go to the library today as it's closed.

Anna: Oh no, I wanted to get some books. I have an exam Monday and I really need to study. Do you know when it reopens?

Shira: I think it's open again tomorrow. You could try the library on the other side of town if you need the books today.

Anna: Good idea! Do you want to come with me?

Shira: Yes, I'll be ready in an hour. I need to drop off some books. My exams finished yesterday.

Anna: Oh wow, lucky you. I still have three more to do.

2 🎧 6.9 Listen to the conversation again. Cross out the consonants that are not pronounced.

3 Work with a partner. Read the conversation from Exercise 1. Remember the areas of catenation and elision you identified.

Speaking task

As a group, discuss ways to reduce pressure students face.

Brainstorm

Look at these possible ways to reduce the pressure facing students. Check (✓) your opinion of each idea.

	Great idea	Good idea	Not a bad idea	Terrible idea
Ask for less homework.	☐	☐	☐	☐
Create a schedule.	☐	☐	☐	☐
Get advice from parents.	☐	☐	☐	☐
Get advice from peers.	☐	☐	☐	☐
Get a part-time job.	☐	☐	☐	☐
Hire a private tutor.	☐	☐	☐	☐
Participate in a sport.	☐	☐	☐	☐
Spend less time with friends.	☐	☐	☐	☐
Take easier classes.	☐	☐	☐	☐
Take fewer classes.	☐	☐	☐	☐

Plan

1 Work with a partner. Choose the best ideas from the chart about how to reduce pressure on students. Be sure you can support your opinions.

2 Prepare for your discussion. You can use these questions below.

What types of pressure do students face? How can different types of pressure affect us?
What causes different types of pressure? How can we best deal with the pressure we face?

Speak

Join another pair. Discuss your ideas. If you have any advice for others, try and use a conditional sentence with a modal. If you don't know the word for something, try explaining it.

Share

Share the best ideas from your group with the class.

Reflect

How easy or difficult would it be to reduce the pressures you face?

Review

Wordlist

MACMILLAN
DICTIONARY

Vocabulary preview

call sb sth (phr v)	exact (adj) **	psychological (adj) **
compete (v) ***	expectation (n) ***	reasonable (adj) ***
demand (n) ***	left out (phr v)	reduce (v) ***
direct (adj) ***	logical (adj) **	support (v) ***
disappoint (v) **	outline (v) **	
distract (v) *	peer (n) **	

Vocabulary development

get behind someone	get good grades	get in trouble	get started
	get in touch	get nowhere	get the message
get going			

Academic words

depression (n) **	instance (n) ***	psychology (n) **	sex (n) ***
factor (n) ***	occur (v) ***	revise (v) *	specific (adj) ***

Academic words review

Complete the sentences using the words in the box. Change the word form where necessary.

complement	factor	revise	specific	tense

1 Bad weather was a contributing _____ to the plane crash.

2 I need to _____ the figures in my report. They're wrong.

3 My best friend and I have very different personalities but we _____ each other well.

4 When you write about a topic, you need to include _____ information about it.

5 Everyone felt very _____ before the exam results were announced.

Unit review

Listening 1	☐	I can listen for how opinions are supported.
Listening 2	☐	I can listen for cause and effect.
Study skill	☐	I can get the most out of a discussion.
Vocabulary	☐	I can use a range of expressions with *get*.
Grammar	☐	I can use modal verbs in conditional sentences.
Speaking	☐	I can explain something I don't know the word for.

Discussion point

Discuss with a partner.

1 What else happens to your body when you're afraid?

   When I'm afraid my mouth gets dry / I can't move / I feel hot.

2 What do you think are the most common fears?

   I think the most common fears are the fear of … and …

3 When was the last time you were afraid? What happened?

   The last time I was afraid was …

How fear works

Our memory of fearful experiences allows us to recognize potential threats. ▶

Our heart pumps blood to our muscles faster because they have to work harder during fight-or-flight responses. ▶

When our muscles become tense, it can cause us to shake.

◀

When we're very afraid, time appears to slow down. It can allow us to remember things in great detail. ▼

▲ The hair on our neck and arms may stand up. This may have helped our hairier ancestors appear larger to potential threats.

VIDEO

SLIP SLIDING AWAY

Before you watch

Before you watch, match the words to the correct definitions.

1 **acrophobia** (n)   a brave and taking risks

2 **daring** (adj)   b very scary

3 **nerve-wracking** (adj)   c a fear of heights

4 **skyline** (n)   d view of the tops of tall buildings in a city

5 **vertigo** (n)   e feeling sick and dizzy and think you might fall

UNIT
AIMS

LISTENING 1 Recognizing organizational phrases
LISTENING 2 Listening for problems and solutions
STUDY SKILL Increasing confidence when speaking

VOCABULARY Suffixes -ful and -less
GRAMMAR The present perfect tense with adverbs
SPEAKING Managing questions

A scared skydiver.

While you watch

Read the questions. Watch the video and choose
T (True) or *F* (False).

1   The slide is inside a skyscraper.   T / F
2   The slide is made of glass approximately
    3 cm thick.   T / F
3   The glass is used in places that normally
    has hurricanes and earthquakes.   T / F
4   Everyone in the video has a fear
    of heights.   T / F
5   Los Angeles is well-known for its
    tall buildings.   T / F

After you watch

Answer the questions with a partner.

1   Do you have any phobias?
    Yes, I hate …
    No, I'm not afraid of … (+ noun / + -ing)

2   How would you feel if you went on this slide?
    I'd feel …
    I would be …

3   Why do you think they built this slide?
    It could be because …
    One reason could be …

Fear of public speaking

A Vocabulary preview

1 Match the words in bold with the correct definitions.

a A large **audience** gathered to hear the president speak.

b In order to deliver a successful speech, you have to **connect** with your audience.

c The disagreement between the two speakers does not **involve** you.

d I have to **limit** the number of facts in my talk so that there aren't too many.

e I'm really nervous about this talk. I need to **memorize** a lot of information.

f The professor gave a **speech** on the power of positive thinking.

g **Athletes** often have to work hard to manage pressure and stay focused on their competitions.

h I'm having a hard time deciding on a **topic** for my class presentation.

1 _____ (n) people who are good at sports, especially athletics, and take part in sporting competitions

2 _____ (n) a subject that you speak or write about

3 _____ (v) to show a relationship between one person or thing and another

4 _____ (v) to learn something so that you remember it perfectly

5 _____ (n) a formal event when someone speaks to a group of people

6 _____ (adj) to prevent a number, amount, or effect from increasing past a particular point

7 _____ (v) to include something or someone as a necessary part of an activity or event

8 _____ (n) the people who come together to watch a movie, hear someone speak, etc.

2 Answer the questions with a partner.

1 Do you think it's a good idea for a student to involve their audience during a presentation?

I think / don't think it's a good idea because …

2 What tips would you recommend for someone who's giving a speech in public for the first time?

I'd recommend that the person practice a lot and …

B Before you listen

1 How do you feel about speaking to these people in English? Mark each one 1 (very afraid), 2 (a little afraid), or 3 (not afraid at all).

____ a native speaker I know well   ____ a native speaker I don't know well

____ a small group in my English class   ____ a large group in my English class

2 Did you mark anything 1 or 2? Were they for any of the following reasons, or another reason? Tell a partner.

> I'm afraid of making grammar mistakes.
> I'm afraid my pronunciation won't be clear.
> I'm afraid I won't know the right word to say.
> I'm afraid I won't understand what people say.

I'm a little afraid to speak to a large group. I guess I'm afraid I'll speak too slowly.

C Global listening

Organizational phrases help introduce important points in a logical way. Listen for these phrases to better understand how the listening text is organized and when the main ideas will be introduced. Some useful phrases include:

In the introduction

Today, I'm going to talk about …   *First, I'll discuss …*

Then, I'll consider …   *At the end of my talk, I'll mention …*

In the main body

Let's now turn to …   *Another important point is …*

In the conclusion

In conclusion, I'd like to summarize …   *The main points I discussed were …*

🎧 **7.1 Number these sentences 1–7 in the order you think you will hear them. Then listen to the talk *Fear of public speaking* and check your answers.**

a Let's now look at the five tips for facing this fear. ____

b Then I'll provide five tips for facing this fear. ____

c Today I'm going to talk about the fear of public speaking. ____

d So, here are three facts about the fear of public speaking. ____

e First, I'll discuss three interesting facts about public speaking. ____

f Let me conclude by providing you with some additional information. ____

g At the end of my talk, I'll tell you where you can get more information on this topic. ____

Listening for details

D Close listening

1 🎧 7.1 Listen to *Fear of public speaking* again. Complete the notes with words in the box. Three words are not used.

| audience | equally | facts | fear | main | men | memorize | negative |
| prepared | question | speak | stress | time | tips | women |

Fear of public speaking

[1] _____

    1. Number 1 [2] _____*; more common than dying*
     75% of people have this fear
    2. Men and women affected [3] _____
     [4] _____ *more likely to find ways to deal with this fear*
    3. Can have [5] _____ *effect on career*

[6] _____ *for facing this fear*
    1. Start small—will begin to feel confident
    2. Be prepared—practice and [7] _____ *yourself*
    3. Don't [8] _____ *everything—the* [9] _____ *points are enough*
    4. Reduce [10] _____ *—do what works for you*
    5. Involve the [11] _____ *—talk to them, make eye contact, take questions*

Additional info
Recommended reading: Be [12] _____, *Be Confident by Dr. Ricardo Lopez*

2 🎧 7.2 Listen to six excerpts of students asking questions. Match each from the talk to how the speaker handles it.

Question 1	a He gives some examples.
Question 2	b He gives a personal opinion.
Question 3	c He talks about a personal experience.
Question 4	d He says he has already answered the question.
Question 5	e He answers by saying what experts have said.
Question 6	f He says he doesn't know the answer.

E Critical thinking

Which of these are good / bad ideas for someone who has a fear of public speaking?

Use note cards.	Film yourself.	Practice speaking into a mirror.
Include jokes.	Join a public speaking club.	Watch successful speakers.

Pronunciation for listening

Listening for conversation fillers

Fillers are words and phrases that carry little to no meaning in conversation. They fill gaps in speech and are not usually stressed. They are often said quickly and may sound like a single word. It's good to be able to recognize fillers so that when they appear in conversation, you know to ignore them and focus on the meaningful content. Some common fillers include:

and um	*and just*	*so like*	*I mean*
you know	*you see*	*kind of*	*or something*

1 Look at the sentences from *Fear of public speaking* and underline the fillers.

1 But I'm not nervous today, you know.

2 So, like, how small should the group be?

3 Also, have more material in case you finish early—I mean, not a lot, just a little extra.

4 I think it's kind of boring for the audience.

5 You see, for many, the minute just before you speak is the most fearful.

6 And, um, how do you do that?

2 🎤 7.3 Listen and check (✓) the speaker who uses a conversational filler. (The filler is not included here.)

1 ☐ A: How did you find the lecture?
  ☐ B: It was pretty interesting.

2 ☐ A: How can I get over my fear of public speaking?
  ☐ B: Why don't you practice your presentation in front a mirror?

3 ☐ A: I've always been terrified of snakes.
  ☐ B: What do you think causes that?

4 ☐ A: What are your fears? What are you afraid of?
  ☐ B: I'm not afraid of much, but I don't like driving fast.

5 ☐ A: How do you deal with your fear of flying?
  ☐ B: I listen to music and try not to think about it.

6 ☐ A: I'm terrified of crowded places. What can I do?
  ☐ B: Well, it's not something you can get over right away.

3 🎤 7.4 Listen and write the sentences you hear. Do not include any filler words.

1 _____.

2 _____.

3 _____.

4 _____.

Phobias

A Vocabulary preview

1 Match the words in bold with the correct definitions.

1	**awful** (adj)	a	afraid
2	**certain** (adj)	b	bad; terrible
3	**control** (n)	c	to make something less good or effective
4	**frightened** (adj)	d	to succeed in dealing with a problem
5	**impair** (v)	e	to ask for or try to get something
6	**overcome** (v)	f	the power to make decisions about something
7	**powerless** (v)	g	not able to control or prevent something
8	**seek** (v)	h	having no doubt that something is true

2 Complete the sentences with the correct word from Exercise 1.

1 Sally was very _____ when she saw the spider on her bed.

2 Brandon felt _____ when he got lost in the forest and couldn't find his way out.

3 Fatima is _____ her fear of heights won't stop her from reaching the top of the mountain.

4 I have a fear of large spaces. I feel uncomfortable entering the lecture room. It's _____!

5 When Emiko sees a snake, she has no _____ over her actions.

6 It's OK to _____ help for your fear of public speaking. I'm happy to help you.

7 Before you can _____ a fear, you first need to face it. Ignoring it won't help.

8 My phobia of spiders doesn't seem to _____ my ability to work at the zoo.

B Before you listen

Activating prior knowledge

Look at the pictures below. Which of these things are you most / least afraid of?

storms	snakes	shots	elevators

C Global listening

🔊 **7.5** Look at the common fears below. Listen to the first half of *Phobias* and circle the fears mentioned in the lecture. There are four which are not mentioned.

elevators   exams   heights   open spaces
public speaking   snakes   spiders   the dark   water

D Close listening

When you listen to problems being discussed, you will often need to decide if the solutions suggested are good ones. Listen for phrases like to these to identify the problem and solutions.

Stating problems

Some people have a problem with …

One problem many people face is …

Offering solutions

One thing you can do is …

I suggest …

When listening to solutions, listen critically. Try to determine if the solutions have well-supported arguments or reasons behind them.

1 🎧 7.5 Listen to the first half of *Phobias*. Answer the questions.

1 What is Dr. Kristin Patterson an expert on?

_____

2 Why is a reasonable fear of something a good thing?

_____

3 How do people react when faced with a phobia?

_____

4 What was Dr. Patterson's patient Maggie afraid of?

_____

5 Why was it important that she face this phobia?

_____

2 🎧 7.6 Listen to the second half of *Phobias*. How did the doctor solve Maggie's problem with elevators? Check (✓) the solutions. There are three which are not mentioned.

☐ realizing she needed help

☐ physical exercise

☐ talking about what scared her

☐ watching the elevator

☐ holding her breath in the elevator

☐ taking the elevator up one floor at a time

☐ techniques to help her relax

☐ deep breathing

☐ closing her eyes

☐ standing in the elevator

☐ taking the elevator up only one floor

☐ taking the elevator to the tenth floor

E Critical thinking

Discuss these questions in a group.

1 Which of Dr. Patterson's techniques do you think are good? Why?

The techniques that I think are good are … because …

2 What is something you are afraid of? Do you think you have a phobia?

I'm afraid of …   I think / don't think I have a phobia because …

Study skills — Increasing confidence when speaking

These tips can help you increase your confidence when speaking:

1 **It's OK to be nervous** Turn the negative feelings into positive energy.
2 **Organize your thoughts** Know what to say and why you want to say it.
3 **Slow down** Speak slowly and pause to let your audience take in what you've said.
4 **Keep it simple** When you speak, don't try to cover everything.
5 **Say something** Your ideas will be helpful to those around you.
6 **Act confident** People can't tell if your heart is beating quickly, so don't tell them.

© Stella Cottrell (2013)

1 Read what these presenters said. What tip in *Increasing confidence when speaking* did they follow? Write the number.

a I wasn't sure that people would like my presentation. But the audience seemed to enjoy what I said. ____

b I knew what I wanted to say and why I thought it was important. I created an outline so I could present my ideas in a logical way. ____

c I felt nervous before I started. I closed my eyes and tried to turn that feeling into something more positive. It worked! ____

d My topic was hard to understand, and I had a lot to say about it. But I tried to make it really simple. For example, I used easier words. ____

e I didn't feel very confident. My hands were sweaty and I thought about making a joke about that. But I decided to just *act* really confident. ____

f I thought if I spoke fast it would show I knew a lot, but then I decided it was better to present my ideas slowly, to give the audience time to think. ____

2 Answer the questions with a partner.

1 How confident are you when you speak in your first language? When you speak English?

2 Think of a person who speaks confidently. What makes this person confident?

Vocabulary development

Suffixes -*ful* and -*less*

Two common suffixes you can add to words to make adjectives are -*ful* and -*less*. The suffix -*ful* means "full of" (fearful = full of fear) while -*less* means "without" (fearless = without fear). For some words, either suffix can be added. For others, you can use one suffix but not the other.

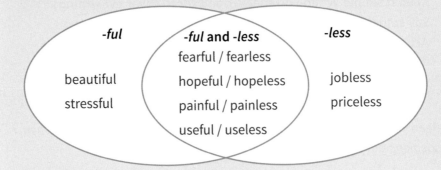

-ful
beautiful
stressful

-ful and *-less*
fearful / fearless
hopeful / hopeless
painful / painless
useful / useless

-less
jobless
priceless

1   Which words in the box take -*ful*, which take -*less*, and which can take either? Write the complete words in the diagram.

care   harm   help   point   power   truth   wonder   worth

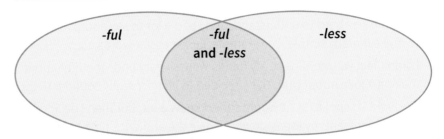

-ful   *-ful* and *-less*   *-less*

2   Write the correct word with the suffix -*ful* or -*less* to complete the sentences.

fear   harm   home   point   stress   success   wonder

1   It's _____ to be here. I'm so happy you invited me.

2   A phobia is more than being _____ of something.

3   A snake's bite can make you very sick. They are very _____.

4   I find exams really _____. I can never sleep the night before.

5   After a lot of hard work, Hassan was _____ in finally overcoming his fear of flying.

6   I tried to make Beth understand, but it was _____. She wouldn't listen.

7   After Keith lost his job, he worried that he would become _____.

Academic words

1   Match the words in bold with the correct definitions.

1	**affect** (v)	a	by machine; without people doing anything
2	**author** (n)	b	something you can use to help you achieve something
3	**automatic** (adj)		
4	**definition** (n)	c	to influence something to change
5	**impact** (n)	d	a way of doing something using a special skill
6	**resource** (n)	e	a statement of what a word means
7	**survey** (n)	f	someone who writes books, articles, etc.
8	**technique** (n)	g	a set of questions that you ask a large number of people
		h	an effect or influence

2   Complete each question with the correct word from Exercise 1.

1   What _____ would you recommend for someone who wanted to relax more?

2   Who is your favorite book _____?

3   Do you think a fear of something could have a serious _____ on someone's life?

4   Are you able to give a _____ of the word *fear*?

5   Do you think your fears can _____ your friendships?

6   If a researcher asked you to take a 30-minute _____, would you do it?

7   What _____ would you look at if you wanted to know what *fright* means?

8   Do you think _____ taxi doors that open for customers is a good idea?

3   Choose four questions from Exercise 2. Ask and answer them with a partner.

A: *Do you think _____ taxi doors that open for customers is a good idea?*

B: *I do. I think it shows good service.*

Speaking model

You are going to learn how to use the present perfect, how to pause and vary your speaking speed, and how to manage questions. You are then going to use these skills to give a presentation on a problem you've had to solve.

A Analyze

1 Read the model and add the sentences in the correct places.

a Does anyone have any questions?

b Then I'll tell you the techniques I have used to solve it.

c In conclusion, speaking to others has had a very positive impact on my life.

d Soon people started to talk to me more.

e No one talked to me, and I didn't talk to anyone.

> Today I'm going to talk to you about a problem I had recently. First, I'll describe the problem. ¹___ In summary, I have found it very difficult to make friends at this college. The problem started on the first day of class. I was very nervous because I didn't know anybody here. I felt very alone and I was worried I wouldn't make new friends.
>
> On the first day of class, I sat by myself. ²___ I didn't know what to do. Other people spoke to each other—just not to me. I realized if I wanted things to change, I needed to make the effort to make friends. After a few days, I started small conversations with other students. I said hello, talked about the classes, and asked questions. ³___ I also joined some clubs, like soccer and English conversation. It took a while, but I have made several good friends that way, especially in the English conversation club.
>
> ⁴___ It's only November but I have already made plenty of friends. I haven't met any other new students yet, but when I do I'll definitely talk to them. I know first-hand how not having friends can affect you and how scary a new environment can be. In fact, I'm so busy now that I still haven't had time to call my old school friends to see how they're doing in their new college!
>
> ⁵___

2 How does the speaker organize his presentation? Number 1–4.

___ He asks if the audience has any questions.

___ He presents his problem.

___ He explains his problem in more detail.

___ He summarizes what he is going to say.

3 Underline where the speaker uses *have* + verb. Is he talking about something that happened now, or in the past?

B Discuss

Answer the questions with a partner.

1 Summarize how the speaker handled the problem.

2 Have you ever had a problem like the speaker describes? What did you do?

Grammar

The present perfect tense with adverbs

Use the present perfect tense to talk about an event or experience at an unspecified time in the past. The exact time is unknown or unimportant. We often use adverbs with the present perfect. Note each adverb's placement.

Adverb	Placement	Example
still	before *has / have*	I **still** haven't finished my report.
already	before the past participle	I have **already** chosen my topic.
ever	before the past participle	Have you **ever** spoken in public?
never	before the past participle	I have **never** spoken in public.
yet	at end of question	Have you prepared your talk **yet**?
not … yet	at end of sentence	I haven't prepared my talk **yet**.

1 Rewrite the sentence or question with the adverb in the correct place.

1 Sally has given that speech three times. (already)

_____

2 Have you seen a 10-centimeter-long spider? (ever)

_____

3 Jeff hasn't practiced his talk. (yet)

_____

4 I haven't spoken with a doctor about my fear of heights. (still)

_____

5 Have they taken their final exams? (yet)

_____

6 They have felt comfortable in small, closed spaces. (never)

_____

2 Rewrite the sentences using the present perfect and the correct placement of the adverb.

1 Samantha (**upload** / **already**) a video of her talk.

_____

2 Glenn (**not tell** / **yet**) anyone about his fear of flying.

_____

3 Iris (**not share** / **still**) her fears with her friends.

_____

4 I (**not meet** / **never**) anyone with a fear of cats.

_____

Speaking skill

Managing questions

When you give a presentation or talk, you can take questions as you speak or leave time at the end for questions. Let your listeners know that you expect questions.

Stating you will take questions as you speak

Let me know if you have any questions.
If you have any questions, feel free to ask.

Stating you will take questions at the end

Please hold all questions until the end.
I'll be happy to answer any questions later.

Taking questions at the end

I'd be happy now to take a few questions.
Let's open it up and see if you have any questions.

You don't have to answer every question. If you answered it already, refer quickly to what you said. If you can't answer a question, it's best to be honest about it and say so.

Referring back to a previous point

I believe I answered that question previously.
I think I've already answered that.

Stating you don't know the answer

I'm afraid I don't know.   *I'm sorry, but I don't have the answer to that.*

1 🎧 7.7 Listen to three excerpts from *Fear of public speaking*. How does the speaker manage questions? Complete the sentences.

 1 **Speaker**: Let's get started. If you have _____.

 2 **Student 5**: Do you know when that book was published?
    Speaker: _____ the answer to that. I'll try and find out.

 3 **Student 6**: Yes. Why shouldn't someone memorize a presentation?
    Speaker: I think _____.

2 Work in a group. You have five minutes to prepare a three-minute talk on one of the topics below. Say you will take questions at the end. Then answer any questions.

foods that are good for the brain	how to deal with urban sprawl
the best way to deal with peer pressure	what *emotional nourishment* means
why people should do community service	a comparison of two companies

Pronunciation for speaking

Pausing and pacing

Briefly pausing between chunks of language can help you sound confident and natural while presenting, and will stop you from running out of breath. It allows the audience time to take in what you are saying.

Unnatural pausing

Everyone has certain fears, # which is normal # and a good thing, # because a reasonable fear # of something dangerous # helps keep us safe.

Natural pausing

Everyone has certain fears, which # is normal and # a good thing, because # a reasonable fear of # something dangerous helps # keep us safe.

In the first sentence, the pauses are natural and effective because they occur between chunks of language that exist as stand-alone ideas. In the second sentence, they sound unnatural and the speaker might seem nervous. It would also be a lot harder to understand.

As with pausing, pacing can be a very effective technique. Don't always speak at the same speed. Instead, vary your speaking speed. In general, speak slower when making your most important points, and speak faster when using less meaningful language.

1 🎧 **7.8** Listen to an excerpt from *Phobias*. Notice how the speaker pauses (#) for effect.

First, # she had to face her fears. # After talking about her fears, # ¹ ⟶_____ and after learning to relax, # she started to watch the elevator. # In the beginning, # she just watched people getting on, # ²_____ getting off, # smiling, # and talking with others. # ³_____ The next day, # she watched it again. # But then we stepped in the elevator, # together. # It didn't go anywhere # we just let the doors open and close automatically. # She was nervous, # ⁴_____ but by breathing deeply and relaxing, # she was in control. # ⁵_____ The next day, # we repeated the first two steps, # and then finally took the elevator up, # but only one floor. # We repeated this over several days, # ⁶_____ adding one floor each day.

2 🎧 **7.8** Listen again. Add ⟶ arrows where the speaker talks faster. Add ⟵ arrows where the speaker talks slower. The first one is done for you.

3 Practice reading the text from Exercise 1 to a partner. Did you pause and use quick and slow pacing in the same places?

Speaking task

Give a presentation on a problem you have had to solve.

Brainstorm

Work with a partner. Think of some problems you have had that you were able to solve, using the ideas in the box. Discuss the problems and how you tried to solve them.

a fear you overcame	a time you repaired a broken friendship
a difficult choice you made	something you had trouble learning to do

Plan

1   Choose one problem. Take notes answering the questions in the problem and solution boxes below. Then take notes on the steps you took to solve the problem and the result(s).

Problem		Solution	
Who? What? When? Where?		*Who? What? When? Where?*	
How? Why?		*How? Why?*	
Steps taken	*Results*		*End result*

2   Use your notes to prepare a presentation on your topic. Consider where you could pause and when you may want to speak faster or slower.

Speak

Work in groups. Take turns presenting your topic to your group. Let your audience know you expect some questions during or after your presentation. Pause and vary your speaking speed to make your presentation as clear and effective as possible.

Share

Share and discuss what you liked about each presentation.

Reflect

Reflect on your presentations with a partner.

Was public speaking like this a stressful experience?
How comfortable were you?
Were the tips in the unit helpful?
What would you do differently next time?

Review

Wordlist

**MACMILLAN
DICTIONARY**

Vocabulary preview

athlete (n) *	connect (v) ***	involve (v) ***	powerless (adj)
audience (n) ***	control (n) ***	limit (v) ***	seek (v) ***
awful (adj) **	frightened (adj) **	memorize (v) *	speech (n) ***
certain (adj) ***	impair (v)	overcome (v) **	topic (n) ***

Vocabulary development

beautiful ***	homeless *	powerful/	truthful
careful/careless	hopeful/hopeless	powerless	useful/useless
fearful/fearless	jobless *	priceless	wonderful ***
harmful/harmless	painful/painless	stressful	worthless
helpful/helpless	pointless	successful ***	

Academic words

affect (v) ***	automatic (adj) **	impact (n) ***	survey (n) ***
author (n) ***	definition (n) ***	resource (n) ***	technique (n) ***

Academic words review

Complete the sentences using the words in the box.

definition   impact   resource   survey   technique

1 A dictionary will give the part of speech and pronunciation of a word as well as its _____.

2 The government's _____ revealed that most people drive to work.

3 Making a mind map of your ideas is a useful _____ to help you plan an essay or project.

4 A country's people are its most important _____.

5 The economic situation made a huge _____ on the sales results last year.

Unit review

Listening 1		I can recognize organizational phrases in speech.
Listening 2		I can listen for problems and their solutions.
Study skill		I can be confident when I am speaking.
Vocabulary		I can use prefixes and suffixes with -ful and -less.
Grammar		I can use the present perfect tense with adverbs.
Speaking		I can invite and manage questions when giving a talk.

The Science of Storytelling

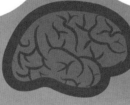

From a young age, our brains start to recognize stories as a group, or pattern, much like colors or shapes.

When you listen to a story, the way you think and feel become similar to the way the storyteller thinks and feels.

Stories are very effective because your brain processes them the same way as reality.

With facts, you use two parts of the brain. With stories, you use multiple parts, including your senses.

Your brain releases a chemical into your system when it experiences an emotional event, which makes it easier to remember.

Discussion point

Discuss with a partner.

1 What is a story you remember from your childhood? What happened in it?

I remember a story called … In the story, …

2 Do you prefer to read, write, listen to, or tell stories? Why?

I prefer to … stories because …

3 What's the last story you read, heard, or saw in a movie? What was it about?

The last story I read / heard / saw was … It was about a girl who …

VIDEO

THE FRENCH SPIDERMAN

Before you watch

Discuss with a partner what you might see or hear in the video using the prompts below.

drink water   safety gear   slippery   vertigo   the weather   a wheel

The video might be about a person who …

LISTENING 1 Listening for the order of events
LISTENING 2 Adding details to a diagram
STUDY SKILL Finding your creative streak

VOCABULARY Using descriptive adjectives
GRAMMAR The past progressive
SPEAKING Using sentence adverbs

Shoshone Bannock, a native American Indian, holding a wooden cane.

While you watch

Read the sentences. Watch the video and complete them with the missing words.

1 Alain, "The French Spiderman", was climbing a rotating _____.

2 Alain doesn't usually wear _____ when he climbs up buildings.

3 Alain is nervous about _____ conditions.

4 The rain makes the building wet and _____.

After you watch

1 Imagine you are going to tell a friend about this news story. What do you remember? Make notes.

1 Where does the story take place?
2 Who are the characters?
3 Is there a problem the main character faces?
4 If so, how does she solve the problem?
5 What's the most exciting part of the story?

2 Share your answers with a partner.

A travel story

A Vocabulary preview

1 Match the words in bold with the correct definitions.

1	**afford** (v)	a	to be late for something, e.g., a train, and not get it
2	**counter** (n)	b	in a way that is clear to see or understand
3	**curious** (adj)	c	wanting to find out about something
4	**obvious** (adj)	d	a stamp in your passport that allows you into another country
5	**miss** (v)	e	a long, flat table where customers are served
6	**reserve** (v)	f	to arrange for a room or seat for future use
7	**system** (n)	g	to have enough money to pay for something
8	**visa** (n)	h	a set of connected things that work together

2 Complete each sentence with the correct word from Exercise 1.

1 If you _____ your flight, you should have to buy a new ticket.

2 People who work at the check-in _____ at the airport have difficult jobs.

3 If you need a _____ for another country, it should be free.

4 Being _____ about other people is a good quality to have.

5 Plane tickets should be cheaper so more people can _____ to fly.

6 It is _____ that the best way to travel these days is by train.

7 It's a good idea to _____ a hotel a month in advance.

8 It's important for a plane to have an entertainment _____ on long flights

3 Work with a partner. Which sentences do you agree with? Give your opinion.

B Before you listen

1 Work in a group. Describe your last vacation.

On my last vacation, I went to … with …

2 Work in a group. Have these things ever happened to you on a trip? What happened?

got lost   had terrible weather   got sunburned

When I went to …, unfortunately I got lost in …

C Global listening

1 🎧 8.1 Listen to *A travel story*. Check (✓) the things Rachid mentions in this story.

- [ ] how long his conference was
- [ ] how he got to the airport
- [ ] why he was late for the airport
- [ ] something he forgot to pack
- [ ] how much he paid the driver
- [ ] where he sat on the plane
- [ ] what he ate on the plane
- [ ] the weather in London

2 Choose the best summary of the story.

a Rachid almost missed his flight to London. He thought he lost his passport but found it in his bag at the airport.

b Rachid missed a flight to London because he forgot to pack his passport. He went home to get it and took a later flight.

c Rachid missed his flight to London twice. The first time he forgot he needed a visa. The second time he forgot his passport, so he was too late for the flight.

Listening for the order of events

D Close listening

Stories are usually told in chronological order—the order in which the events happened. Listen for these expressions to help you follow the story.

*First, ...   Then ...   After that, ...   Next, ...   Finally, ...   Later, ...
The next day, ...*

first event   second event

*First, he called to say he was running late. **Then** he called again to say he was getting gas.*

Be careful of the following expressions. They indicate one event happened before another.

Earlier, ...   Previously, ...   Before, ...   Prior to that, ...

second event   first event

*I changed money into the local currency. I had already confirmed my seat **the night before**.*

1 🎧 8.2 Listen to the first part of the story *A travel story*. Number the events from 1–6 in the order they happened.

- ☐ a He got a visa.
- ☐ b He made sure his flight was confirmed.
- ☐ c He went home to get his passport.
- ☐ d He called to book a taxi.
- ☐ e He bought a plane ticket to London.
- ☐ f He changed money.

2 🎧 8.3 Listen to the rest of *A travel story*. What happened next? Complete the notes.

1 He _____ his flight. ⟩ **2** A _____ helped him get on a new flight. ⟩ **3** He got his _____ stamped. ⟩ **4** He _____ for a few hours.

8 He got to his _____ in time. ⟨ **7** He flew to London _____ class. ⟨ **6** A man asked him to _____ seats. ⟨ **5** He found out he had a tiny _____ seat.

E Critical thinking

Rachid is a good storyteller. Do you agree with this statement? Why / why not?

Study skills | Finding your creative streak

Creativity is especially important for generating ideas in the early stages of new assignments. You can use more logical approaches later, to evaluate which creative idea is best.

Approaches that help creativity happen:

- "Play"

Select any two random objects. Find as many connections between them as you can (e.g., by size, color, owner). How could you apply this type of play to your coursework?

- Find what you are looking for
- There's more than one right answer
- Combine things
- Metaphor

Take an issue out of academic context and see what it looks like in the world.

© Stella Cottrell (2013)

GLOSSARY

metaphor (n) a word or phrase that means one thing and is used for referring to another thing in order to emphasize their similar qualities

1 Read *Finding your creative streak*. Work with a partner to answer the questions creatively. Use at least one of the suggested words in your sentence.

Example: Why are stories important?

warnings   wisdom   community   memory

Stories are important because they can bring a community together.

1 What makes a good story?

connect   imagine   place   feeling

_____

2 What makes a good storyteller?

quality   experience   passion   listener

_____

3 How can stories affect how we feel?

change   emotion   power   meaning

_____

4 How can the ability to tell a good story help you in life?

job   confidence   natural   speaking

_____

2 See how many ideas you can generate by completing these sentences.

1 Writing an essay is like making a cake because …
2 Study is like a game of soccer because …
3 Being a student is like being a sandwich because …

3 Compare your ideas from Exercise 2 with a partner.

Elements of a plot

A Vocabulary preview

1 Match the words in bold with the correct definitions.

 a The **climax** of the story was when the fight happened.

 b Demands from friends can create a **conflict** for some people.

 c Are you **familiar with** Haruki Murakami's books?

 d The writer's simple words made it easy for me to **follow** the story.

 e There are some computers that can translate **literary** works.

 f I love reading so I plan to study **literature** in college.

 g The main **plot** of the story is the man's journey to India.

 h The **setting** of the play is an old farm house in 1950s Canada.

 1 _____ (n) stories, poems, and plays, especially those considered to have value as art

 2 _____ (n) a time or place in a book, movie, play, etc.

 3 _____ (adj) a series of events that make up the main story

 4 _____ (n) the most exciting or important moment in a story

 5 _____ (n) involving books or the activity of writing, reading, or studying books

 6 _____ (phrase) to know about something because you learned or heard about it before

 7 _____ (v) to understand something by reading or listening

 8 _____ (n) a situation in which it's difficult for two things to exist at the same time

2 Answer the questions with a partner.

 1 What is the last novel you read? What was the plot? Was there a conflict?

 2 What North American literary writers are you familiar with?

 3 What is the greatest work of literature in your native language? Why do you like it?

B Before you listen

Activating prior knowledge

Work with a partner. Think of a story you both know well. Then discuss and take notes on these questions. You will use these notes later in the unit.

1 Where does the story take place?

2 Who are the characters?

3 Is there a problem the main character faces? If so, how does he or she solve the problem?

4 What's the most exciting part of the story?

C Global listening

1 🎧 8.4 Listen to *Elements of a plot*. Add the five elements to the correct places on the diagram.

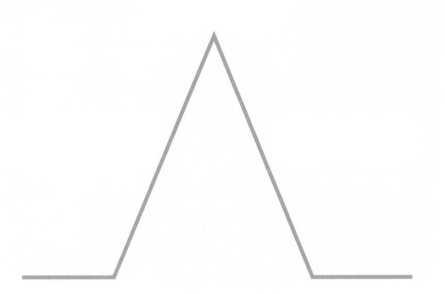

Freytag's Pyramid

2 Write each element from Exercise 1 with its correct explanation.

1 ——————— = The characters are introduced.

2 ——————— = The "plot thickens."

3 ___Climax___ = It's the high point of the story.

4 ——————— = The character deals with the conflict.

5 ——————— = There is no more conflict for the hero.

D Close listening

Always pay attention to any diagrams or charts a presenter shows. These may already give you clues to what the main points of the lecture will be, and they might help you see the content more clearly. You can quickly copy diagrams into your notes, adding more detailed notes while you listen.

1 🎧 8.4 Listen for one more important detail for each element. Add the details to the diagram in *C Global Listening* on page 141.

2 Use your answers from Exercise 1 to complete the notes below.

Freytag's Pyramid = [1]_____ *elements to most stories*
- *Exposition = character &* [2]_____ *introduced; initial conflict is also introduced*
- *Rising action = plot thickens; main character faces a* [3]_____ *; tension builds up*
- *Climax = high point, main events + the most* [4]_____ *part of story*
- *Falling action = character deals with the conflict; we see* [5]_____ *of character's actions*
- *Resolution =* [6]_____ *tension than before, no more conflict, our Qs are* [7]_____

3 🎧 8.5 You will hear five parts of a short story out of order. Listen and number the parts 1–5 in the order they are mentioned.

Exposition ___   Rising action ___   Climax ___   Falling action ___   Resolution ___

4 🎧 8.6 Listen to the correct order of the story and check your answers.

E Critical thinking

Discuss these questions in a group.

1 Look back at the notes you wrote for the story you discussed in Before you listen. Describe how the story follows / doesn't follow the five elements mentioned in the listening.

I think the story follows / I don't think the story follows the five elements. It …

2 Can you think of any stories that don't follow the order of the five elements?

I saw a movie that showed the resolution first. It was called …

Pronunciation for listening

> ## Emphatic stress for storytelling
>
> In order to tell a story creatively and interestingly and to keep the audience's attention, storytellers often emphasize descriptive words, such as adjectives (*huge, crazy, tiny*) and adverbs (*really, totally, extremely*). The words we emphasize illustrate the most unusual / exciting aspect of the story we are telling.
>
> Notice the change in emphasis in the second of each pair of sentences:
>
> *I was starting to get extremely **WORRIED**.*
> *It was definitely the most **EXCITING** part.*
>
> *I was starting to get **EXTREMELY** worried.*
> *It was **DEFINITELY** the most exciting part.*

1 🎧 **8.7** Listen to the sentences. Underline the word that receives emphatic stress.

1 *The Boy Who Cried Wolf* is a really famous story.
2 The boy was obviously lying to the people in town.
3 The boy was extremely embarrassed by his actions.
4 The wolf's teeth were enormous!
5 The people in town totally didn't believe the boy.
6 The boy learned a huge lesson that day.

2 🎧 **8.7** Now listen again and repeat to a partner.

3 Add an adjective or adverb in the box to each sentence.

| awful   extremely   long   obviously   tiny   totally |

1 When I listened carefully, I could hear a _____ voice through the door.
2 The old man told us something that was _____ unexpected.
3 After such a _____ day at work, all I wanted to do was put my feet up.
4 There was an _____ smell coming from under the bed.
5 _____, my friend and I told the police everything we had seen.
6 Suddenly an _____ angry-looking elephant ran toward us.

4 Work with a partner. Practice saying the sentences in Exercise 3. Place emphatic stress on the words you added.

Vocabulary development

Descriptive adjectives

You can make what you say much more interesting by not using the same adjectives all the time. Try to use more descriptive language. For example, instead of saying a room is *very dirty*, you could say it's *filthy*. From that, your audience will build a picture in its mind. A good thesaurus or dictionary can help build your vocabulary and your use of descriptive adjectives.

1 Match the words on the left to the words with the closest meaning.

1	**happy**	a	down
2	**cold**	b	exhausted
3	**tired**	c	freezing
4	**clean**	d	ancient
5	**sad**	e	thrilled
6	**old**	f	pure

2 Look at each word in bold and the four words that follow. Cross out the word that does not belong.

1	**nice**	kind	friendly	strange	helpful
2	**big**	massive	plain	enormous	huge
3	**good**	excellent	pleasant	curious	great
4	**bad**	amazing	awful	horrible	terrible
5	**pretty**	ugly	lovely	attractive	beautiful
6	**small**	tiny	little	loud	baby-sized

3 Rewrite these sentences using one of the words from Exercise 2.

1 The service at our hotel was bad. _____

2 The lion's eyes were big. _____

3 A nice woman showed me how to find the mall. _____

4 The weather on our trip was good. _____

5 The restaurant served small food portions. _____

6 We saw one pretty sunset after another. _____

Academic words

1 Match the words in bold with the correct definitions.

1 **accommodation** (n)	a	something unusual or exciting that happens
2 **analysis** (n)	b	the money used in a particular country
3 **confirmed** (adj)	c	having been established or made firm, often used with *flight* or *hotel*
4 **currency** (n)		
5 **drama** (n)	d	a house, apartment, or hotel room
6 **element** (n)	e	the nervous feeling you have when reading or watching something exciting
7 **fee** (n)		
8 **tension** (adj)	f	the study of something in detail to better understand it
	g	an important, basic part of something
	h	an amount of money that you pay to be allowed to do something

2 Complete the sentences with words from Exercise 1.

1 When you travel, do you book your _____ online?

2 I wanted to change the date of my trip, but the _____ was so high I decided not to.

3 What _____ do they use in Switzerland—francs or euros?

4 There was a lot of _____ between the hero and his friend in the story.

5 I made sure I had a(n) _____ flight before I went to the airport.

6 The main _____ of this story is the fight between the two brothers.

7 There was so much _____ in the book that I couldn't stop reading it.

8 The airline study included a(n) _____ of recent accidents.

3 Answer the questions with a partner.

1 What currency do you use in your country?
   We use …

2 In which of the five elements of story is there the most tension?
   I think the most tension occurs during …

3 Is it important for you to have confirmed accommodation before you travel?
   Confirmed accommodation is / isn't important to me because …

Speaking model

You are going to learn about using the past progressive tense, pronouncing /k/ and /g/ sounds at the beginning and end of words, and sentence adverbs. You are then going to use these skills to tell a story.

A Analyze

1   A student is telling a story. Complete the model with the time expressions.

> a few months ago   finally   the next day   the week before   then

This happened to me [1]_____. I came home from work, exhausted after a long day. [2]_____, I had ordered a new pair of shoes. I really needed them because I was going to my brother's wedding [3]_____.

When I got home I saw a note on the door. Someone had tried to deliver something. They couldn't because I wasn't home. There was a phone number, so I called and asked to have it delivered. I was [4]_____ able to relax a bit because I knew I had everything I needed for the wedding.

I cooked dinner and started to watch a movie. After a few hours, I heard the doorbell ring. I went to the door expecting to see a delivery person holding a box. I saw a boat in my yard instead! I didn't know what to say. I just laughed. The delivery person just smiled. I told him I was waiting for shoes. He checked the order and realized they had made a mistake in the order number. The shoes were on a nearby delivery truck. He took away the boat and told me to wait. [5]_____, at midnight, I heard my doorbell again. It was the same man, holding my box.

2   Are any elements of Freytag's pyramid missing from the story?

B Discuss

Answer the questions with a partner about the story.

1   Is this a funny, happy, scary, or embarrassing story? What in the text helped you decide?

   This is a … story. The word … makes this clear.

2   What do you like about the story? What don't you like?

   I like the part about …

   I don't like when …

Grammar

The past progressive

Form	Example
was / were + present participle	*I was starting to get extremely worried.*

You can use the past progressive to describe an event that was in progress in the past. It is often used to provide the background of a story or event.

It was raining that morning.   *The taxi driver was running late.*

Why were you talking to your teacher?

When recalling a story or experience, we often use the past progressive and simple past together. The action described by the simple past interrupts the action described by the past progressive.

I was running when I fell.   *I fell when / while I was running.*

1 Complete the sentences with the past progressive form of the verbs in parentheses.

  1   We _____ (climb) a hill yesterday at noon.

  2   Sarah _____ (write) her book report around 11:00 p.m. last night.

  3   Mark and I _____ (watch) TV when we heard about the news.

  4   It was a beautiful day. The sun _____ (shine) and the birds _____ (sing).

2 Complete these sentences with the simple past or past progressive form of the verb in parentheses.

  1   While we _____ (wait) for the bus it _____ (start) to rain.

  2   When I _____ (get) home last night my roommate _____ (sleep) on the sofa.

  3   Something _____ (fall) on my head while I _____ (walk) under the bridge.

  4   They _____ (hurry) to the airport when they _____ (have) a car accident.

3 Work with a partner and take turns asking and answering the questions. Try to use a mix of the past progressive and simple past in your answers.

  1   Why were / weren't you at school this morning?

  2   What were you doing yesterday?

  3   Where were you going last night?

Speaking skill

A sentence adverb expresses the writer or speaker's attitude toward the thought being expressed. They usually occur at the beginning of a sentence. They are commonly used when telling stories.

Obviously, I asked the driver to go back to my house.

Clearly, I was starting to get really worried.

Luckily, there was one seat left.

Thankfully, I made my flight.

1   Match the sentence adverb to when it is used.

1	basically	a	when emphasizing that what you are saying is true
2	clearly	b	when talking about the most important aspects of something
3	honestly		
4	hopefully	c	when saying something is apparent to most people
5	luckily	d	when saying something is unusual
6	strangely	e	when saying you want something to happen
7	surprisingly	f	when saying something happens in a good or lucky way
8	thankfully		
9	unfortunately	g	when saying you are pleased something unpleasant is not happening
		h	when expressing that something is disappointing
		i	when saying something happens in an unexpected way

2   Circle the correct sentence adverbs. Then practice saying the sentences.

1   This book is about two people in a new relationship. **Basically / Luckily**, it's a love story.

2   I hated that book. **Honestly / Hopefully**, I can't understand why it was so popular.

3   I only had one day to read the novel. **Thankfully / Obviously**, I was able to finish it.

4   That movie scared many of the adults in the audience. **Unfortunately / Clearly**, it's not for children.

5   I got to the airport really late! **Luckily / Strangely**, I still made my flight.

Pronunciation for speaking

/g/ versus /k/

The sound /g/ as in *bag* is almost the same as the sound /k/ as in *back*. To pronounce /g/ touch your throat. Say /g/. You will feel vibration. Now say /k/. You shouldn't feel a vibration. These sounds are easier to tell apart and pronounce at the beginning of words (e.g., *goat* vs. *coat*) than at the end of words.

1   Work with a partner. Choose and say one word in each pair. Your partner spells the word he or she hears.

gap / cap   guard / card   coal / goal   gold / cold

bag / back   log / lock   bug / buck   league / leak

2   Underline the /g/ sounds and circle the /k/ sounds. Then practice the sentences with a partner.

1   I put my bag on the seat next to me.
2   He called again to say he was getting gas.
3   I finally got to the airline check-in counter.
4   I never put it back in my bag.
5   I called to book a cab.

3   🎧 8.8 Listen again to this part from *The Boy Who Cried Wolf*. Underline all the /g/ sounds and circle all the /k/ sounds. Then practice reading the excerpt aloud.

There was once a young boy who lived near a dark forest. Every day he had to take care of his sheep. The young boy was lonely and bored.

He decided on a plan to relieve his boredom. He ran into the village shouting, "Wolf! Wolf!" People came to help but there was no wolf. This amused the boy so he did it again. Again, there was no wolf so the people walked away.

Soon after that, a wolf really did come into the village and began eyeing his sheep. He was extremely frightened. He cried, "Wolf! Help! This time, there really is a wolf!" The wolf came closer and closer to his sheep.

Speaking task

Prepare and tell a story of your choice.

Brainstorm

1   Work with a partner. Think of a possible story for each type. It can be a true story that happened to you, a story you heard or read, or something you imagine.

a funny story   a happy story   a scary story   an embarrassing story

2   Choose one of the stories. Make notes on all the events that happened, in order.

1	_____	6	_____
2	_____	7	_____
3	_____	8	_____
4	_____	9	_____
5	_____	10	_____

Freytag's Pyramid

Climax

Rising Action   Falling Action

Exposition   Resolution

Plan

1   Create a Freytag's Pyramid for your story and add your notes from Exercise 1 to the correct parts of the diagram.

2   Work with your partner. Show each other your diagrams. Do you agree on the division of the parts? Suggest any details to make the stories clearer or more interesting.

Speak

Work in groups. Tell your stories. Include descriptive adjectives and sentence adverbs in your stories. Use emphatic stress to make your story interesting to the listener.

Share

Decide on the most interesting story in each group. Share it with the class.

Reflect

Which story was the most interesting? Why?
What was challenging for you when you told your story?
The stories in this unit use words. What are some other ways to tell stories?

Review

Wordlist

MACMILLAN
DICTIONARY

Vocabulary preview

afford (v) ***	curious (adj) **	literature (n) ***	reserve (v) ***
climax (n) *	familiar with something	miss (v) ***	setting (n) ***
conflict (n) ***	follow (v) ***	obvious (adj) ***	system (n) ***
counter (n) **	literary (adj) **	plot (n) **	visa (n)*

Vocabulary development

ancient	enormous	helpful	massive
attractive	excellent	horrible	pleasant
awful	exhausted	huge	pure
baby-sized	freezing	kind	terrible
beautiful	friendly	little	thrilled
down	great	lovely	tiny

Academic words

accommodation (n) **	confirmed (adj)	drama (n) ***	fee (n) ***
analysis (n) ***	currency (n) ***	element (n) ***	tension (adj) ***

Academic words review

Complete the sentences using the words in the box.

analysis   currency   fee   recover   tension

1   The money a country uses is called its _____. In the United States, it's the dollar.

2   The magazine article provided a detailed _____ of the election.

3   The sum students pay for their tuition is called the tuition _____.

4   Fred will _____ from his illness soon.

5   There is a lot of _____ in this dramatic story.

Unit review

Listening 1 ☐ I can listen for the order of events.

Listening 2 ☐ I can listen for details and put them on a diagram.

Study skill ☐ I can be creative.

Vocabulary ☐ I can use a range of descriptive adjectives.

Grammar ☐ I can use the past progressive.

Speaking ☐ I can use adverbs to show my attitude.

Discussion point

Discuss with a partner.

1 Which fact surprises or worries you the most? Why?

The fact about ... surprises / worries me because ...

2 Do you use more or less of the following things as you did five years ago?

electricity   gas
paper   plastic

I use more / less / the same amount of ...

Our *environment* by the *numbers*

Recycling one drinks can can save enough energy to run a TV for **three hours**.

Each time you open the refrigerator, **30%** of the cold air escapes.

27,000 **trees** are chopped down every day for toilet paper.

Every day, U.S. businesses use enough paper to fly around the Earth **20 times**!

Plastic thrown into our oceans kills about a **million** sea creatures every year.

84% of all household waste can be recycled.

VIDEO

solar box

GOING GREEN

Before you watch

Match the phrasal verbs in bold with the correct definitions.

1 **come up with**   a   transform

2 **pop up**   b   represents

3 **run out of**   c   appear

4 **stands for**   d   think of a plan or invent a solution

5 **turn into**   e   have nothing left (e.g. no battery power, no milk left in the fridge)

UNIT AIMS

LISTENING 1 Listening for pros and cons
LISTENING 2 Listening to a presenter interact with an audience
STUDY SKILL Preparing a poster

VOCABULARY Environment word families
GRAMMAR Modal passives
SPEAKING Interacting with a presenter

A woman in Pakistan steps on recyclable plastic bags in Lahore.

While you watch

Read the statements. Watch the video and choose
T (True) or *F* (False).

1 Phoneboxes in London are all red.   T / F
2 The Solarbox uses solar power.   T / F
3 Two Spanish men invented the Solarbox.   T / F
4 Kirsty thinks London is not an
   environmentally-friendly city.   T / F
5 Harold says phones and apps are getting
   bigger and using more power.   T / F

After you watch

Answer the questions with a partner.

1 Is the city that you live in environmentally friendly?
2 Do you think it is important to have
   environmentally friendly chargers for phones?

   Yes, it is very important because …

   No, I don't think it is so important because …

3 What other "green" inventions would work well in a
   city?

Solar power

A Vocabulary preview

1 Match the words in bold with the correct definitions.

1 **dishwasher** (n)
2 **fuel** (n)
3 **install** (v)
4 **panels** (n)
5 **renewable** (adj)
6 **solar** (adj)
7 **store** (v)
8 **supply** (v)

a a type of energy that replaces itself by natural processes, e.g., through sunlight

b flat pieces of material (e.g., glass) that form part of something else

c to make something available to someone

d relating to the sun

e a substance (e.g., gas, oil, wood) that makes heat when burned

f a machine that washes dishes

g to put a piece of equipment somewhere so it's ready to use

h to keep for future use

2 Complete each sentence with the correct word from Exercise 1.

1 Drivers can easily save _____ by simply driving slower.

2 If you only turn your _____ on when it's completely full, you won't need to use it as often.

3 The problem with _____ energy is that it's expensive to _____ it for later use.

4 If you want to _____ your home with clean energy, consider _____ sources such as wind power.

5 It's easy to _____ some _____ on your roof to get energy from the sun.

3 Work with a partner. Which sentences do you agree with? Give your opinion.

B Before you listen

Activating prior knowledge

Which of these types of energy do you think is the most environmentally friendly? Why?

gas   oil   solar   water   wind

C Global listening

🎧 **9.1** Listen to *Solar energy*. Answer the questions.

1 Why are Aicha and Steven talking about solar energy?

 a They are preparing for a class debate.

 b They have to create a poster on its pros and cons.

 c They need to decide whether solar energy is a good or bad idea for their school.

2 Which description best describes Aicha's position?

 a There are many good reasons to use solar energy.

 b Solar energy may be OK for some people, but not for everyone.

 c Solar energy is just a trend and will not be used much in the future.

3 Which description best describes Steven's position?

 a Solar energy is only for rich people in rich countries.

 b There are many disadvantages to solar energy.

 c We shouldn't spend money on solar energy but instead invest in wind power.

4 Who uses facts and statistics to support their opinion?

 a Aicha

 b Steven

 c both Aicha and Steven

Listening for pros and cons

D Close listening

Speakers will often discuss both the pros (arguments *for*) and the cons (arguments *against*) an issue. Considering both sides is a useful way to find a solution. If you are aware that both sides of an issue will be discussed, take notes in two columns. Speakers may choose to discuss all the advantages first, and then all the disadvantages, but usually one advantage is mentioned, followed by one disadvantage, and this order continues throughout the argument.

9.1 Listen to *Solar energy* again. Complete the notes.

Pros	Cons
1 solar energy is renewable—will always have it	1 sunlight not always available, e.g., night and cloudy days; some places get little sun in winter
2 capacity to store solar power using _____	2 batteries are large, heavy, and _____
3 can get to many places without electricity	3 not effective when air is bad/polluted
4 _____ and friendly to environment (no pollution)	4 pollution caused by _____ + moving solar power systems
5 reduces energy costs -> people can _____ extra	5 initial setting-up costs can be _____
6 panels getting _____, easy to maintain, last a long time	6 businesses need a lot of _____ to set up solar panels
7 _____	

E Critical thinking

Discuss these questions in a group.

1 In general, do you view solar energy as a positive or negative thing? Why?
   I view solar energy positively / negatively because …

2 What do you think is the main reason the world is not using more solar energy? What could world leaders do to encourage solar energy use?
   I think the main reason is …   We could …

3 What would happen if solar power became the only power source?
   One thing that would happen is …

Study skills   Preparing a poster

Students are often asked to give presentations in order to start off a class discussion, provide a variety of perspectives, or develop a skill required by many professions. If you are using a poster, …

make it large, bright, and informative

use blocks of text under large numbered headings

avoid putting too much in the poster

make it clear which order to read the information.

© Stella Cottrell (2013)

1   What are some other things that you think a good poster should have?

2   Work with a partner. According to the ideas in the box above, what is good about this poster? Make any changes to the poster that you think will improve it.

Wind power advantages vs. disadvantages

Pros

Clean energy
keeps the atmosphere clean

Less space
turbines require less space than a power plant

Renewable
we'll always have wind!

Reach
can reach people in far-off locations

Cons

Less power
wind power creates less electricity than other fuels

Costs
turbines are expensive to build

Wild life
each turbine kills four birds a year

Noise pollution
similar to a small jet airplane

Did you know?
A single wind turbine can power 500 homes.
Unlike other types of power, wind uses no water.
98.7% of wind turbines are installed on private land.
Wind turbine technician is one of the fastest growing jobs in the U.S.

Eco-tourism

A Vocabulary preview

1 Match the words in bold with the correct definitions below.

a It would be **beneficial** to the environment if you recycled plastic.

b She drove over the flowers in my garden **by accident**.

c **Keep** these three things **in mind** when you decide to hike in the spring.

d If we don't **preserve** our lakes and river better, it could affect our water.

e We hiked to a very **remote** area where we couldn't see any city lights at night.

f I've always wanted to go on a **safari** in Africa to see wild elephants.

g All of us need to be more **sensitive** to the damage our lifestyles cause.

h It would be interesting to work in the **tourism** industry because I like to travel.

1 _____ (n) a journey to see or photograph wild animals

2 _____ (adj) far away from towns, cities, or people

3 _____ (adj) something that has a good effect or influence on someone or something

4 _____ (n) the business of providing services to travelers

5 _____ (v) to care for a place in order to protect it from harm

6 _____ (adj) showing that you care about something

7 _____ (phrase) without being planned or intended

8 _____ (phrase) to remember something, especially something important

2 Answer the questions with a partner.

1 Would you be interested in working in the tourism industry? Why / why not?

2 What is one thing you could do to help preserve our natural world better?

3 What would be important to keep in mind when camping in a remote area?

4 What is one way we could be more sensitive to the damage to the environment our lives cause? How would it be beneficial?

B Before you listen

Activating prior knowledge

Rank these activities 1–4 in the order they interest you. Then compare with a partner. How eco-friendly are they?

☐ you feed sharks from a boat in South Africa

☐ you learn about traditional medicine in Brazil

☐ you ride a Jet Ski™ in the United Arab Emirates

☐ you stay in a tree house in Malaysia's rainforest

C Global listening

1 🎧 9.2 Listen to *Eco-tourism*. Number the parts of the poster from 1 to 8 in the order they are presented.

Listening to order information

___ # Eco-tourism

___ **Eco-tourism is …**
tourism that sends people to mostly untouched parts of the world.

___ **It aims …**
to show that tourism does not need to harm nature or traditional culture.

___ The good	___ The bad
It helps preserve nature.	It can damage nature.
It creates jobs for local people.	There is little control over it.
It allows people to see more of the world and its cultures.	It changes cultures, even when we don't want it to.

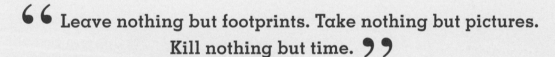

❝ **Leave nothing but footprints. Take nothing but pictures. Kill nothing but time.** ❞

___ **Tips**
- Don't accept everything you hear or read.
- Do your homework.
- Check the group size.
- Make sure companies follow the rules.
- Make sure local people benefit.
- Make sure the accommodation is built from renewable materials.

2 Choose the best subtitle for the poster.

a Top eco-tours of the year

b Why eco-tours are a waste of money

c Think twice before you go on an eco-tour

Listening to a presenter interact with the audience

D Close listening

A speaker who is giving a presentation may choose to interact with the audience. When the speaker interacts with the audience, it helps them to know that the information that follows is important and should be listened to.

Inviting someone to listen

Can I tell you a bit about …?

Would you like to hear about …?

Referring to a visual

As you can see here, … /
Do you see that …?

Notice in this box / picture / graph that …

Further explaining an idea

Let me just add that …

To say a bit more about that, …

Offering additional information

I can provide you with a list of sources.

I'm happy to send you a link to …

1 🎧 9.3 Listen to four excerpts from *Eco-tourism*. Number in order from 1 to 4 the ways the presenter interacts with the audience.

☐ She invites someone to listen.　　☐ She further explains an idea.

☐ She refers to a visual.　　☐ She offers additional information.

2 🎧 9.4 Listen to another excerpt. Match each tip to how the presenter expands upon it.

1 Don't accept everything you hear or read. ___

2 Search for reviews of companies online. ___

3 Check the group size. ___

4 Make sure companies follow the rules. ___

5 Ensure that local people benefit. ___

6 Make sure the accommodation is built from renewable materials. ___

a She gives a reason.

b She gives examples.

c She encourages us to ask questions.

d She states what she does.

e She asks us to imagine something.

f She asks us to remember something.

E Critical thinking

Discuss these questions in a group.

1 Do you think the pros outweigh the cons of ecotourism? Why / why not?

I think / don't think the pros outweigh the cons because …

2 If you were interested in an eco-tour, what questions would you ask the company?

I would ask …

Pronunciation for listening

Linking vowel sounds between words

When one word ends with a vowel sound and the next word begins with a vowel sound, a speaker may add a /j/ or /w/ sound between them. If the speaker's lips are wide and open when the first vowel sound is pronounced, they add /j/. When they are more rounded and closed, they add /w/.

say anything	see it there	high and low	I know it	go away	too often
/j/	/j/	/j/	/w/	/w/	/w/

1 🎧 9.5 Listen to these sentences from *Solar energy*. What sound is added between the underlined words? Circle /j/ or /w/.

1 It's really important that we practice.   /j/ /w/
2 That's how our debate will probably go.   /j/ /w/
3 Solar energy is the future.   /j/ /w/
4 And I know at least several reasons we should use it more.   /j/ /w/
5 There may be only seven hours of sunlight a day there.   /j/ /w/
6 They are the size of a dishwasher or small washing machine. /j/ /w/
7 You can save up to a hundred dollars a month.   /j/ /w/
8 So are we prepared for tomorrow?   /j/ /w/

2 Each of these sentences from *Eco-tourism* contains an added /j/ or /w/ sound between two words. Circle the two words. Then write the sound below it.

1 Can I tell you a little bit about my poster?
2 Any money or fees that a tourist pays goes back into the community.
3 Eco-tourism can allow us to see more of the world and its cultures.
4 This is good for people who are in urban environments as well as locals.
5 An example of that is Africa, where many people go on safari to see wild animals.
6 See if the money goes directly to helping local communities.

Vocabulary development

Environment word families

When you learn a verb, try and learn its noun form at the same time. When you learn a noun, learn its verb form. Some verbs become nouns by adding -ment (*advertise/advertisement*). Some becomes nouns by adding -tion (*protect/protection*). Some verbs and nouns have the same form (*appeal/ appeal*). There are multiple ways to form nouns, so it's best to check a dictionary.

1 Work with a partner. Complete the chart with the correct verb or noun form.

Verb	Noun	Verb	Noun
argue	argument	6 _____	question
1 _____	attraction	pollute	7 _____
conserve	2 _____	8 _____	power
3 _____	damage	9 _____	preservation
develop	4 _____	produce	10 _____
5 _____	installation	11 _____	supply

2 Complete the questions with verbs or nouns from Exercise 1.

1 Is air _____ a problem where you live?

2 Have you ever had an _____ with someone about the environment?

3 Do you think your country should use more solar or wind _____? Why?

4 What is one thing you could do to _____ energy at home?

5 What is a place in your country that tends to _____ a lot of tourists?

6 Do you think that a company will someday _____ a plane that runs only on solar energy?

7 What type of transportation does the most _____ to the environment?

3 Work with a partner. Ask and answer the questions from Exercise 2.

Academic words

1 Match the words in bold with the correct definitions.

1	**capacity** (n)	a	certain
2	**convert** (v)	b	the possibility to develop or achieve something in the future
3	**data** (n)		
4	**definite** (adj)	c	to change from one use or method to another
5	**fees** (n)	d	the ability to do something
6	**guarantee** (n)	e	facts and information used for making calculations
7	**potential** (n)	f	money you get from working or investing money
8	**relevant** (adj)	g	relating to something in an appropriate way
		h	a promise that something is true

2 Complete the sentences with words from Exercise 1.

1 There is a _____ link between the burning of fossil fuels and climate change.

2 Climate change has the _____ to have very serious effects.

3 The warnings from scientists about climate change 20 years ago are still _____ today.

4 You are never too old to change your habits. Everyone has the _____ for change.

5 People who drive big cars should have to pay more in _____ because they use so much fuel.

6 We need something that allows us to _____ our garbage and other waste into fuel.

7 There is no _____ that buying green products helps the environment.

8 The _____ on climate change is clear. The fact is it's real and happening now.

3 Work with a partner. Which of the statements from Exercise 2 do you agree with? Which do you disagree with? Support your opinions.

Speaking model

You are going to learn about using modal passives, word stress, and the language needed to interact with a presenter. You are then going to use these skills to conduct a poster presentation.

A Analyze

1 A student is presenting the poster from page 157. Complete the presentation with these phrases and sentences.

> Let me just add that   I'm happy to send you a link   As you see here on this poster
> Notice in this picture that   Would you like to hear about wind power

Excuse me, ma'am. Hello, sir. ¹_____? Great! Thank you. ²_____, I have listed both pros and cons. There are four advantages. First, wind power is clean. It's an energy source that can be used to help keep our air clean. Second, wind power doesn't use a lot of space. In fact, wind turbines use less space than a power plant. ³_____ the turbine doesn't use much space at all. Another advantage of wind power is that we'll always have it. Wind is a renewable energy source unlike fuels like oil and gas. Finally, wind power is able to reach people in far-off, remote places.

There are some disadvantages to wind power, though. Wind does not create as much power as other fuels. Also, the cost of building wind turbines is high. ⁴_____ turbines are expensive, but keep in mind that they are an investment and you will have them for a very long time. Another con is that each wind turbine kills about four birds a year. So they aren't always great for animals. Oh, you'd like to know my source of that fact? Of course. ⁵_____. The last disadvantage I want to mention is that wind power is noisy, so noise pollution might be viewed as a concern by some people. Some say the noise is similar to that of a small jet engine.

2 What words does the speaker use to signal he is moving on to the next part?

B Discuss

Answer the questions with a partner.

1 In what order does the speaker present the parts of the poster?
   First, the speaker talks about …

2 Does the speaker give enough detail about the pros and cons?
   I think the speaker gives / doesn't give enough detail about …

3 What question would you ask the presenter?
   I would ask the presenter what / how / why …

Grammar

Modal passives

Form	Example
modal + *be* + past participle	*Solar panels can be placed on the roof.*

The passive voice may be used to describe actions when the person performing the action is unknown, unclear, or unimportant. When we use the passive voice, it can make some sentences sound less direct and more polite.

It is common to use modals in passive sentences:

A lot of money could be saved by installing solar panels.

A large amount of space may be needed for solar panels.

Something should be done about climate change.

People shouldn't be allowed to go on safaris in the morning.

Solar panels should be checked regularly.

1 Complete the sentences with modal passives.

   1 The eco-hotel might _____ (finish) in three months.

   2 Many eco-tourism companies can _____ (find) in Costa Rica.

   3 The topic of climate change should _____ (teach) in all grade levels.

   4 Extra electricity from solar power could _____ (sell) to others.

   5 Our rain forests have to _____ (save) for future generations.

   6 The city's regular taxis may _____ (replace) by electric taxis.

2 Rewrite these sentences using modal passives.

   People shouldn't waste food.

   Food shouldn't be wasted.

   1 You have to follow the rules in the national park.

   _____

   2 People can find great eco-tourism deals online.

   _____

   3 People should put their computers to sleep at night.

   _____

   4 You can't pay for the eco-tour with a credit card.

   _____

3 Answer the questions with a partner.

   1 Should solar panels on office roofs be required by law?

   2 What needs to be done to stop global warming?

Speaking skill

When you listen to a talk, lecture, or presentation, you may be able to interact with the speaker. Use this opportunity to further question and give feedback on what the speaker is discussing. Use these phrases when appropriate.

Showing interest

That's interesting.

I like that idea.

Asking for clarification

What does this graph/chart/picture represent?

What do you mean by that?

Asking for more details

Can you tell me more about that?

Can you talk a little more about that?

Interrupting politely to ask a question

Sorry, but can I ask a question?

Excuse me. Can I ask a quick question?

1 Match the words to make sentences and questions.

1	That's	a	that idea.
2	I like	b	represent?
3	Can you tell	c	a quick question?
4	What does that graph	d	me more about that?
5	Can you talk a little	e	interesting.
6	Excuse me. Can I ask	f	by that?
7	Sorry, but can	g	more about that?
8	What do you mean	h	I ask a question?

2 🎧 9.6 Listen to four excerpts from *Eco-tourism*. Write what the listener says when interacting with the presenter.

1 _____

2 _____

3 _____

4 _____

3 Work with a partner. Talk for 90 seconds about the pictures on your phone, or an object in your bag. During that time, your partner will try to …

- show interest
- ask for more details
- ask for clarification
- interrupt politely to ask a question

A: This picture is my friend Mattias. He's from Germany.

B: Can you tell me more about him?

A: Sure. He's …

4 Now switch roles.

Pronunciation for speaking

> ## Word stress with word suffixes
>
> When you add a suffix to a word to change its form, its stress pattern may change. The stress often moves to the right.
>
> | Stress moves one syllable over | | Stress moves two syllables over | |
> |---|---|---|---|
> | conSERVE | conserVAtion | SIMilar | simiLARity |
> | eLECtric | elecTRIcity | SENsitive | sensiTIvity |

1   Look at the words in the first column. Underline the stressed syllable.

   1   benefit   beneficial

   2   install   installation

   3   preserve   preservation

   4   electric   electrical

   5   present   presentation

   6   inform   information

   7   prepare   preparation

   8   environment   environmentally

2   Look at the words in the second column from Exercise 1. Underline the stressed syllable.

3   🎧 9.7 Listen and check your answers.

4   Practice saying these sentences with a partner.

   1   If you don't see how buying local products benefits you, think about how it's beneficial to others.

   2   This website on the installation of solar panels will make it easy when you install your own.

   3   If our goal is the preservation of forests, we need to preserve a lot more than we currently do.

   4   Something is wrong with our electricity because our electrical appliances aren't working properly.

   5   I always want to present first so I can then relax and listen to the other presentations.

   6   If you care about the environment, you should try and buy environmentally friendly products.

Speaking task

Present a poster on the environment.

Brainstorm

1 Work with a partner.
   Student A: You will present the poster on page 157. You will listen to a presentation of the poster on page 161.
   Student B: You will present the poster on page 161. You will listen to a presentation of the poster on page 157.

2 Look at the poster you are going to listen about. Write the following.

   a question that asks for more details:

   _____?

   a question that asks for clarification:

   _____?

   a question you might want to ask on the topic:

   _____?

Plan

Now look the poster you are going to present. Decide the order you want to present the information. Take notes on the following.

when you will refer to the poster: _____

ideas in the poster you might further explain: _____

additional information you might offer a listener: _____

Speak

1 Take part in a poster presentation session.
   Student A: Invite Student B to listen to your poster presentation. Present the main ideas of the poster. Use your notes from the Plan section to help you.
   Student B: Approach Student A and accept the offer to view the presentation. Show interest in what the speaker says. Ask your question from your brainstorm section at an appropriate time.

2 Now switch roles.

Share

Work with your partner. Say what you liked about each other's presentation.

Reflect

Which role did you feel more comfortable in: listener or speaker? Why?
What would you do differently if you were to present the poster again?

Review

Wordlist

MACMILLAN DICTIONARY

Vocabulary preview

beneficial (adj) **	keep something in mind (v)	renewable (adj)	store (v) ***
by accident (phrase)		safari (n)	supply (v) ***
dishwasher (n)	panel (n) ***	sensitive (adj) ***	tourism (n) **
fuel (n) ***	preserve (v) ***	solar (adj) **	
install (v) **	remote (adj) **		

Vocabulary development

argue (v) ***	conservation (n) ***	installation (v) **	preservation (n) *
argument (n) ***	damage (v) ***	pollute (v) *	produce (v) ***
attract (v) ***	develop (v) ***	pollution (n) ***	production (n) ***
attraction (n) **	development (n) ***	power (n / v) ***	question (n / v) ***
conserve (v)	install (v) **	preserve (v) ***	supply (n / v) ***

Academic words

capacity (n) ***	data (n) ***	fee (n) ***	potential (n) ***
convert (v) **	definite (adj) **	guarantee (n) **	relevant (adj) ***

Academic words review

Complete the sentences using the words in the box.

affect	capacity	convert	data	potential

1 Yiu has the _____ to be an excellent doctor one day.

2 I want to _____ some dollars into dirhams. What's the exchange rate?

3 We have analyzed the _____ and discovered that unemployment in graduates is up by 8%.

4 The school only has 200 students at the moment, but it has the _____ to take 350.

5 A bad grade in a test might _____ your overall grade at the end of the year.

Unit review

Listening 1		I can listen for pros and cons in an argument.
Listening 2		I can understand when a speaker invites interaction.
Study skill		I can prepare a poster.
Vocabulary		I can make nouns from verbs and verbs from nouns.
Grammar		I can use modal passives.
Speaking		I can interact with a presenter.

10 MEDICINE

THE FUTURE OF MEDICINE

SMARTWATCHES
A smartphone is not very useful for a doctor, but a smartwatch can be used to make calls, send messages, schedule appointments, and view test results.

MEANINGFUL SOCIAL MEDIA
The widespread use of social media makes it possible for doctors and patients to send, share, and store medical information, but only if used properly.

CUSTOMIZED APPS
More and more apps are available, making it more difficult for doctors and patients to choose the right ones. Customized apps would allow patients to choose exactly what they need.

HOME MONITORING
Patients can now check their blood pressure at home. In the future, there will be more ways to monitor your health and send the doctor the results, leading to the early prevention of diseases.

GAMES
Can game-like daily routines and medical therapies lead to a healthier life? Wearable products and online services will lead to better health, but only if games are designed well.

SUPERCOMPUTERS
A supercomputer named Watson can process 200 million pages of data in seconds, which is a huge help for doctors who need to make important medical decisions.

◀ ALREADY AVAILABLE — IN PROGRESS — IN THE FUTURE ▶

Discussion point

Discuss with a partner.

1 Which of the above would you like to use if you were a doctor? If you were a patient?

If I were a doctor / patient, I'd like to use …

2 What is something that is possible in the area of medicine that was impossible ten years ago?

These days it's possible to …

3 What is something you'd like to see happen someday in the field of medicine?

I think it would be good if doctors / patients could …

VIDEO

SEARCHING THE DIRT

Before you watch

Match the words in bold with the correct definitions.

1 **bacteria** (n)
2 **dirt** (n)
3 **genes** (n)
4 **molecules** (n)
5 **treatments** (n)

a part of a cell (that stores the DNA code for life)
b soil or earth from the ground
c something you do or take to cure an illness or injury
d the small unit of something (made of one or more atoms)
e very small living things that sometimes cause disease

UNIT
AIMS

LISTENING 1 Listening to how an argument is supported
LISTENING 2 Listening for speaker attitude
STUDY SKILL Persuading through reasons

VOCABULARY Medical vocabulary
GRAMMAR Indirect questions
SPEAKING Refuting an argument

A girl interacting with a digital heart.

While you watch

Read the questions. Watch the video and choose the correct answer.

1 Why do the two scientists dig up earth?

   a to study the bacteria you find in dirt

   b to find worms to make into medicine

2 What happens when the dirt is taken to a laboratory?

   a the dirt is used to make headache pills

   b the scientists study it to see what bacteria exists

3 Why is it better to use earth from local parks?

   a the scientists don't need to travel to rare environments

   b it will cure people who live locally

After you watch

Answer the questions with a partner.

1 What do you know about medicines that come from plants, animals, and bacteria?

2 Do you think it is important to study dirt and bacteria? Why / why not?

3 If you were a scientist, what would you like to study?

Face-to-face vs. online doctors

A Vocabulary preview

1 Match the words in bold with the correct definitions.

1	**abuse** (n)	a	a feeling of worry
2	**concern** (n)	b	to be important
3	**convenient** (adj)	c	to make someone believe something is true
4	**matter** (v)	d	to copy or move something (e.g., a photo) to the Internet
5	**persuade** (v)		
6	**prescription** (v)	e	the use of something in a dishonest or harmful way
7	**rely on** (phr v)	f	a piece of paper on which a doctor writes the medicine you need
8	**upload** (v)		
		g	easy to do and not causing any difficulties
		h	to trust someone to do something for you

2 Complete each sentence with the correct word from Exercise 1.

1 Nurses should be able to write a(n) _____ for patients.

2 It's not safe to _____ medical records to the Internet.

3 A major _____ of young people is the cost of healthcare.

4 The nurse managed to _____ her manager to give her the day off.

5 The government has done something terrible. It's clearly a(n) _____ of power.

6 It doesn't _____ if you don't tell your doctor the truth about personal things.

7 When you choose a doctor, choose one whose location is _____.

8 It's never good to _____ the opinion of just one doctor.

3 Which of the opinions from Exercise 2 do you agree with? Tell a partner.

B Before you listen

Activating prior knowledge

1 Work in a group. You are going to hear a debate between two pairs of students on which is better: seeing doctors face-to-face or online. Brainstorm possible topics you think the students might discuss.

2 Answer the questions with a partner.

1 How is seeing a doctor online different from seeing a doctor face-to-face?

When you see a doctor online, ... but when you see a doctor face-to-face ...

2 Would you feel more comfortable seeing a doctor face-to-face or online?

I'd feel more comfortable seeing a doctor face-to-face / online because ...

C Global listening

1 🎧 10.1 Listen to *Face-to-face vs. online doctors*. Number the topics from 1–9 in the order the four students discuss them. One topic is not discussed.

Listening for the order of events

___ abuse of the healthcare system

___ accuracy of doctor's assessment

___ dependence on technology

___ how personal the experience is

___ patient privacy

___ access to medical care

___ convenience of getting medical care

___ cost of medical care

___ giving a prescription for medicine

___ getting a second opinion from another doctor

2 Work with a partner. Which of the topics above did you discuss in the *Before you listen* section?

3 Who do you think won the debate? Why?

Listening to how an argument is supported

D Close listening

Look at the ways a speaker can support an argument. Often an argument is supported through a combination of techniques.

Common sense

Everyone knows that …

It's common knowledge that …

Facts and statistics

It's a fact that …

One important statistic is …

Examples and details

For instance, …

Let me give an example …

Expert opinions

According to experts, …

One researcher claims that …

🎧 **10.1** Listen to *Face-to-face vs. online doctors* again. How is each argument supported? Write *CS* (Common Sense), *ED* (Examples and Details), *FS* (Facts and Statistics), or *EO* (Expert Opinions).

1 The only way for a doctor to find out what is wrong is through a face-to-face meeting. ___

2 It's extremely dangerous to write a prescription for any medicine online. ___

3 Nearly two-thirds of patients in the United States said they would see a doctor online. ___

4 People are becoming more worried about their personal information being shared digitally. ___

5 Abuse of the medical system is rising, and it could become an even more serious problem. ___

6 A doctor's charge for a face-to-face meeting may cost $130 to $180, but only $40 to $70 online. ___

E Critical thinking

Discuss these questions in a group.

1 Which side made the stronger arguments? Has your previous opinion about who won the debate changed?

I think … made the stronger argument because …

2 Do you think face-to-face or online doctors are better? Do you agree with the arguments you heard? What helped you agree / disagree?

In my opinion, … are better. The main reason is …

Study skills — Argument: persuasion through reasons

An argument includes:

- a position or point of view
- an attempt to persuade others to accept that point of view
- reasons given to support that point of view.

To identify an argument, it is useful to keep in mind questions such as:

What was the point of producing this text?

What is the main message I am supposed to take from this?

What does the author want me to believe, accept, or do?

What reasons have they offered to support their position?

© Stella Cottrell (2013)

1 Match each position or point of view to what might persuade the listener to accept it.

1 Wellness tourism is only for the rich.

2 It should be the school's responsibility to ensure that children receive regular medical checkups.

3 Medical tourism is a growing industry that we should encourage.

a It brings a lot of money into our country.

b Most people can't take time off for work to travel like that.

c Not all parents have the money to do this on a regular basis.

2 Read the text. Then answer the four questions with your ideas.

Natural medicines and treatments are popular with some groups these days, but there has been little evidence over the years that most natural treatments even work. The positive effects of modern medicine, on the other hand, have been scientifically proven again and again over many years. Without it, we would not have cures for many life-threatening diseases, such as polio and small pox. People who believe that natural treatments will cure them from diseases are not taking this evidence as fact, and are in some cases doing harm to themselves and to others.

1 What was the point of producing this text?

_____

2 What is the main message I am supposed to take from this?

_____

3 What does the author want me to believe, accept, or do?

_____

4 What reasons have they offered to support their position?

_____

Medical tourism

A Vocabulary preview

1 Match the words in bold with the correct definitions below.

a Never take just one doctor's advice. It's best to get one or two **additional** opinions.

b You should go to the doctor's for a **checkup** at least once a year.

c Most problems in the world today are caused by rich, **developed** countries.

d The biggest **drawback** of healthcare programs today is the cost.

e People who go to the hospital receive good **follow-up** care after leaving.

f It's important to have **insurance** in case you ever get sick and can't pay for treatment.

g The Asian **market** is the most important market in the world today.

h People who can't afford it should be given medical **treatment** for free.

1 _____ (adj) extra or more than is usual

2 _____ (adj) occurring after something else

3 _____ (n) the process of providing medical care

4 _____ (n) a feature of something that makes it less useful or interesting

5 _____ (n) a place or group of people that something is sold to

6 _____ (adj) an examination by a doctor or dentist to make sure that you are healthy

7 _____ (adj) describing a place with a lot of industries and business activity

8 _____ (n) an agreement in which you pay a company money and they then pay the costs if you become sick

2 Which of the sentences from Exercise 1 do you disagree with or think are false? Tell a partner.

B Before you listen

Activating prior knowledge

Answer the questions with a partner.

1 Is the medical care in your country good? How often do you get a checkup?

The medical care in … is … I get a checkup …

2 Would you ever consider going overseas for medical treatment?

I would / wouldn't consider going overseas because …

3 What would concern you about receiving medical treatment abroad?

I would be concerned about … because …

C Global listening

 10.2 Listen to the webinar *Medical tourism*. Number the presenter's slides in order from 1 to 6.

GLOSSARY

cardiac (adj) relating to
the heart

☐ DRAWBACKS

1 Lack of follow-up care
2 Malpractice

☐ KEY STATISTICS

- **$50 billion** market (USD)
- **14 million** medical tourists a year
  average cost of **$3,800–$6,000**
  per visit
- worldwide growth of **15%–25%**
  per year

☐ THE TOP FIVE

1 Thailand   4 Singapore
2 Hungary   5 Malaysia
3 India

☐ THE PROCESS

1 person contacts medical tourism
  provider
2 provider asks for a full medical report
3 doctor discusses treatment,
  costs, etc.
4 provider arranges for treatment
  and travel
5 patient pays for treatment
6 doctor says patient can fly home

☐ BENEFITS

1 Lower costs
2 Availability
3 Accessibility (shorter or
  no waiting lists)
4 Quality of care

☐ COUNTRIES

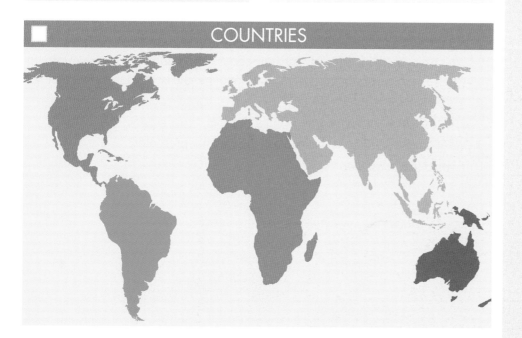

Listening to determine
the speaker's attitude

D Close listening

You can understand a speaker's attitude toward a topic by listening to the specific words they use. Words often have a positive or negative meaning behind them. In these examples, the bold words have a similar meaning, but the speaker feels less happy about what his friends did in the second sentence.

*My friends were **curious** about why I went abroad for my medical treatment.*

*My friends were **nosy** about why I went abroad for my medical treatment.*

In addition, listen to how the speaker speaks. The speaker's tone of voice when they speak about a particular subject also helps to indicate their attitude towards it.

🎧 **10.3** Listen to four excerpts from the webinar. Mark the statements *T* (True) or *F* (False).

1   The speaker thinks the term "medical tourism" is an accurate one.   T / F
2   The speaker thinks the lack of follow-up care is a big problem.   T / F
3   The speaker thinks patients should not receive money from malpractice.   T / F
4   The speaker thinks the issue of doctors treating medical tourists
     but not local patients is something people should think about.   T / F

E Critical thinking

Discuss these questions in a group.

1   Do you think the medical tourism trend is a good thing? Why / why not?
     I think / don't think the medical tourism trend is good because …

2   Which do you think is higher: the number of visitors coming to your country to receive medical treatment, or the number of people from your country going overseas for treatment? Why?
     I think there are more people …

3   What question would you like to ask the webinar presenter?
     I would like to ask her, " …?"

Pronunciation for listening

> ### Linking the same consonant sounds
> When the same consonant sound appears at the end of one word and at the beginning of the next word, it is only pronounced once.
>
> *I'm going to give a short̲talk.*
>
> *They are mu**ch̲ch**eaper than the cost in the patient's home country.*

1 Link the same consonant sounds.

1 But let's̲see if it works.

2 I'll begin now by answering that question.

3 As you can see, it is not tourism exactly.

4 It's simply getting treatment in another country.

5 The amount the patient saves will depend on the country and the treatment type.

6 In these cases, the patient understandably expects some sort of money to be paid back.

2 🎧 10.4 Listen to the sentences and check.

3 🎧 10.5 Listen and complete each sentence with two words.

1 There are many things you can do to _____ _____ illness.

2 Be sure to ask your doctor _____ _____ care is paid for by your insurance.

3 Don't _____ _____ surgery decisions without talking to several doctors.

4 Did you quit your _____ _____ you got new health insurance?

5 I was able to _____ _____ enough time off work for my treatment.

Vocabulary development

Medical vocabulary

1 Match the words in bold with the correct definitions.

1	**clinic** (n)	a	a condition that prevents the body from working properly
2	**cure** (n)		
3	**disease** (n)	b	a short illness that makes you feel hot or cold, weak, and tired
4	**flu** (n)		
5	**home health aid** (n)	c	someone who takes care of someone in their own home
6	**hospice** (n)	d	medicine that helps make a sick person healthy
7	**nursing home** (n)	e	a place where someone goes to receive a particular type of treatment
8	**pill** (n)		
9	**surgeon** (n)	f	a small piece of solid medicine you take with water
10	**therapist** (n)		

g a doctor who performs operations by cutting open the body

h a place that takes care of people who are seriously ill or dying

i a place where older people live who can no longer care for themselves

j someone whose job is to help people with physical or emotional problems

2 Complete the word web with the words from Exercise 1. Think of one more word to add to each box.

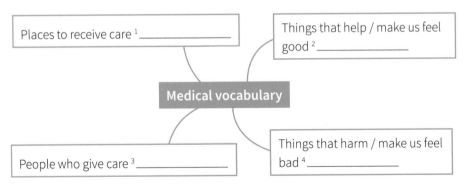

Places to receive care ¹ _____

Things that help / make us feel good ² _____

Medical vocabulary

People who give care ³ _____

Things that harm / make us feel bad ⁴ _____

3 Answer the questions with a partner.

1 Have you ever had the flu? How long did it last?

2 What are three things you can find in a clinic?

3 What kind of person would make a good surgeon?

4 How is a hospice similar to a hospital?

Academic words

1 **Choose the best definitions for the words in bold.**

1 Lifestyle has a bigger impact on health than **gender**.

  a being male or female   b being old or young   c being trained or untrained

2 The hospital staff is requesting additional money to expand their **medical** facilities.

  a relating to pay and other employee benefits

  b relating to how the community views you

  c relating to the treatment of illnesses and disease

3 My doctor said I have two **options** for treating my illness.

  a something free   b something you can choose   c something you don't understand

4 The nurse explained that the **procedure** to help me breathe better would take just ten minutes.

  a a task or operation that can only be done once

  b a task or operation done in a particular way

  c a task or operation that nurses do but doctors don't

5 A **resident** here is able to get medical treatment at reduced rates.

  a someone who needs immediate medical care

  b someone who cannot afford the best care

  c someone who lives in a particular place

6 What **topic** should we discuss in this week's Debate Club?

  a a subject you agree on   b a subject you talk about   c a subject you avoid

7 I have problems with my **vision**, so it's hard to drive at night.

  a not seeing light   b the ability to see   c eyeglasses

2 **Answer the questions with a partner. Explain your answers.**

1 What's an example of a medical procedure?

2 Is it ever a good idea to divide the class according to gender? If so, when?

3 Do you think it's OK for someone to discuss their personal health issues with strangers?

4 What would be an interesting topic to discuss in class?

Speaking model

You are going to learn about asking indirect questions, refuting arguments, and types of stress. You are then going to use these skills to debate.

A Analyze

1 Read these two excerpts from *Face-to-face vs. online doctors.*

Michael: A mistake is more likely to occur when the doctor is only examining you over a video.

Sonia: I don't think that's really true. We believe that an online doctor can see what is wrong with a patient. Not all illnesses of course, but many.

Clarice: Think about how convenient an online doctor can be. With online doctors, they can just send in the information they want. For example, you can send in an image of a skin cut or upload a blood pressure record. This might save you a visit to the doctor's office altogether.

George: It's true that it can be more convenient, but it's also more dangerous. The doctor could give a patient the wrong medicine.

Michael: A patient-doctor relationship is built on closeness and trust. It's impossible to develop that online.

Sonia: I'm afraid that's not accurate. It's not easy, but it is possible. It just takes more time. And I'm not sure patients care about that as much as you think. Do you know what percentage of people are happy to see online doctors? One recent statistic showed that nearly two-thirds of patients in the United States said they would see a doctor online.

Clarice: Seeing a doctor online also means you can get a second opinion more easily. Do you know what a second opinion is?

George: It's when you ask another doctor for his opinion, rather than relying on a single doctor's opinion.

Clarice: Exactly. It's a fact that these days, many insurance companies require them.

2 Underline the two times where the students say the opposing argument is not true / inaccurate. Then circle the two questions. What do you notice?

B Discuss

Answer the questions with a partner.

1 Who do you think makes the strongest argument? Why?

2 Find a statement in the excerpt you think is untrue or inaccurate. What's another way to respond?

I don't think ... is a fact. What is your source for that information?

Grammar

Indirect questions

An indirect question is a question included in another question, such as *Do you know …?* They are less direct, generally more polite, and have a softening effect. Notice that the word order is the same as a statement.

What **is** a second opinion?	<u>Can you tell me</u> what a second opinion **is**?
How many people **see** online doctors?	<u>Do you know</u> how many people **see** online doctors?
How much **did** you **pay** the doctor?	<u>Do you remember</u> how much you **paid** the doctor?

When we ask a yes/no question directly, we add *if*.

Is it the same as wellness tourism?	<u>Can you tell me</u> **if** it **is** the same as wellness tourism?
Does insurance **cost** a lot?	<u>Do you know</u> **if** insurance **costs** a lot?
Did you **win** the debate?	<u>Do you have any idea</u> **if** you **won** the debate?

1 Rewrite these questions as indirect questions.

1 What is a good country for eye care?

Can you tell me _____

2 Does my medical insurance cover hospice care?

Do you know _____

3 When did medical tourism first become popular?

_____

4 Is your second opinion the same as your first opinion?

_____

2 Correct the mistake in each indirect question.

1 Do you know what is the phone number of the hospital?

2 Can you tell me if your doctor take this type of insurance?

3 Do you have an idea how much charges the hospice each day?

4 Can you tell us when will tomorrow's debate begin?

3 Write an indirect question in response to each argument.

1 Medical tourism offers smaller countries an opportunity to make money.

Do you know which countries _____

2 It is easier than ever to find an online doctor who can give you advice.

Do you have any idea how I _____

Speaking skill

To refute an argument, which means to argue against it, you can point out it's not true. Or you can point out that while it may be true, your argument is better. In either case, it's not enough to argue against it—you need to support your argument. Remember, you can do this with logical reasoning, examples and details, facts and opinions.

State the argument you're going to refute

You said that …   You claimed that …   One person reported that …

Say the argument is not true, and why

That's not true because …   I'm afraid that's not accurate since / because …

Say the argument may be true, but yours is better

That may be true, but in fact …   There's some truth to your argument. However, …

1 Match the arguments with the best way to refute them.

1 Hospice care can be expensive.

2 You are more likely to get a cold when it's cold outside.

3 Seeing doctors face-to-face is not very convenient.

4 Drinking a lot of liquids can help you get over a cold.

5 Online doctors are completely ineffective for illnesses that aren't visible, like headaches.

a I'm afraid that's not accurate because I know many illnesses can be detected from a distance.

b There's some truth to that, but many patients feel more comfortable there than a hospital.

c That may be true, but in fact the best way is simply to rest.

d That's not true because there is no evidence of a link with temperature.

e There's some truth to your argument, but I think it's safer because they can examine you up close and not via video.

2 🎧 10.6 Listen and check your answers.

3 Work with a partner. Take turns stating each argument. Say the argument is not true, and why. Or say it may be true, but your argument is better.

1 Natural treatments don't work.

2 Young people don't need medical insurance.

3 You can't trust the medical advice you read on the Internet.

4 Getting a medical checkup once every two years is enough.

You claimed that natural treatments don't work. That's not true because I know people that have felt better after natural treatments.

Pronunciation for speaking

Citation, contrastive, and emphatic stress

Most sentences follow usual stress pattern rules, but there are times when the speaker wishes to add extra stress to a word.

Citation stress: when any word is spoken in isolation, for example when the listener didn't hear you the first time or misunderstood.

*I said **nurse**.*   *I meant **appear**.*

Contrastive stress: when you want to contrast one word with another.

*I went to the doctor on **Tuesday**, not Thursday.*

*I didn't say you could use your insurance. I said you **couldn't**.*

Emphatic stress: when you want to emphasize a certain word, which is usually an adverb or adjective, to show it is surprising or important.

*Medical tourism here is **much** cheaper.*

*My medical bill cost **exactly** $1,000.*

1 🎧 **10.7** Listen and underline the word in each sentence that receives citation, contrastive, or emphatic stress.

   1 We believe that an online doctor can tell what is wrong with a patient.

   2 Yes, I mean, no.

   3 That may be true, but it's a big concern.

   4 What do you mean, no?

   5 In that case, you are spending more money.

2 🎧 **10.8** Underline the words that you think receive citation, contrastive, or emphatic stress. Then listen and check your answers.

   A: These instructions on my prescription are really hard to read. What does this say?

   B: It says p.m. That means evening.

   A: Ah, so I take the medicine in the evening.

   B: Well, not only in the evening. You need to take it in the morning, too.

   A: So I take a pill twice a day.

   B: No, you take two pills twice a day.

   A: OK, thanks. I don't think I need a medical doctor. I need an eye doctor!

3 Work with a partner. Practice the conversation from Exercise 2.

Speaking task

As a group, have a debate on the impact technology has on patient care.

Brainstorm

1 Work in a group. Read the statement. Think about both sides of the issue.

Some people feel that technology improves patient care, while others feel that it doesn't.

2 List all the reasons for each side of the argument that you can think of. Think about:

home health care   wellness tourism   self-monitoring of health

online medical advice   support group chat rooms medical tutorial videos

How technology improves patient care	How technology doesn't improve patient care

Plan

1 Divide your group into two sides. One side will argue that technology helps improve patient care. The other side will argue that technology doesn't improve patient care.

2 Think about supporting points for your side of the argument. Prepare to support your arguments so you can persuade the other side.

3 Think about which arguments and supporting points the other group might use. Prepare to refute the other side's arguments.

Speak

Debate the issue. Make and support your arguments. Refute the arguments of the opposing side.

Share

Join a new group. Summarize what you discussed. Report the main ideas.

Reflect

Reflect on the debate. Discuss these questions with your debate partners.

Was it easier to debate one side of the issue over the other? If so, why do you think that was?

Were you prepared for the other side's arguments? Were they prepared for yours?

If you were to have the debate again, what would you do differently?

How do you think having strong debating skills could help you in the real world?

Review

Wordlist

MACMILLAN DICTIONARY

Vocabulary preview

abuse (n) **	convenient (adj) **	insurance (n) ***	prescription (v) *
additional (adj) **	developed (adj) *	market (n) ***	rely on (phr v) ***
checkup (n)	drawback (n)	matter (v) ***	treatment (n) ***
concern (n) ***	follow-up (adj)	persuade (v) ***	upload (v)

Vocabulary development

clinic (n) **	flu (n) *	nursing home (n) *	surgeon (n) **
cure (n) **	home health aid (n)	pill (n) *	therapist (n) *
disease (n) ***	hospice (n)		

Academic words

gender (n) **	option (n) ***	resident (n) ***	vision (n) ***
medical (adj) ***	procedure (n) ***	topic (n) ***	

Academic words review

Complete the sentences using the words in the box.

guarantee	medical	procedure	residents	vision

1 The operation was a very delicate _____ involving advanced neurosurgery.

2 There is no _____ you will pass your exams unless you make a real effort.

3 If you want to, you can have laser surgery on your eyes to correct your _____.

4 Tom advised his friend to go see a doctor and get some _____ advice for his health problems.

5 Many local _____ object to large new developments in their neighborhood.

Unit review

Listening 1		I can listen for how an argument is supported.
Listening 2		I can listen for a speaker's attitude.
Study skill		I can identify and deal with arguments in a text.
Vocabulary		I can use a range of medical vocabulary.
Grammar		I can use indirect questions.
Speaking		I can refute an argument in a discussion.

Extra material

Unit 1, Speaking task, page 24

Helping the World to Read

- *Donations are used to buy books for children in areas with poor schools.*
- *More than 80% of donations is used to buy and distribute books to children, 15% is used to pay the employees, and 5% is used to help develop the charity.*
- *1,000 employees in the U.S.A.; 500 of which live in affected areas*

Rebuilding Helper

- *Donations are used to rebuild homes, schools, and hospitals after a natural disaster destroys an area.*
- *Most of the donations are used to buy and send supplies to destroyed areas. Employees share 5% of overall profit.*
- *100 employees in the U.S.A., 20 volunteers overseas*

Functional language phrase bank

The phrases below give common ways of expressing useful functions. Use them to help you as you're completing the *Discussion points, Critical thinking* activities, and *Speaking* tasks.

Asking for clarification
Sorry, can you explain that some more?
Could you say that another way?
When you say … do you mean …?
Sorry, I don't follow that.
What do you mean?

Asking for repetition
Could you repeat that, please?
I'm sorry, I didn't catch that.
Could you say that again?

When you don't know the word for something
What does … mean?
Sorry, I'm not sure what … means.

Working with a partner
Would you like to start?
Shall I go first?
Shall we do this one first?
Where do you want to begin?

Giving opinions
I think that …
It seems to me that …
In my opinion …
As I see it …

Agreeing and disagreeing
I know what you mean.
That's true.
You have a point there.
Yes. I see what you're saying, but …
I understand your point, but …
I don't think that's true.

Asking for opinions
Do you think …?
Do you feel …?

What do you think about …?
How about you, Jennifer?
What do you think?
What about you?
Does anyone have any other ideas?
Do you have any thoughts on this?

Asking for more information
In what way?
Why do you think that?
Can you give an example?

Not giving a strong preference
It doesn't matter to me.
I don't really have a strong preference.
I've never really thought about that.
Either is fine.

Expressing interest
I'd like to hear more about that.
That sounds interesting.
How interesting!
Tell me more about that.

Giving reasons
This is … because …
This has to be … because …
I think … because …

Checking understanding
Do you know what I mean?
Do you see what I'm saying?
Are you following me?

Putting things in order
This needs to come first because …
I think this is the most/least important because …
For me, this is the most/least relevant because …

Academic words revision

Units 1–5

Complete the sentences using the words in the box.

> abstract   author   define   eventually   evidence
> furthermore   illustrate   paragraph   participate   strategy

1   I haven't read anything by this _____ before. Is he good?
2   Come to room 12 at 4:00 p.m. and _____ in the debate about the proposed increase in tuition fees.
3   When you write something, start each _____ with a topic sentence.
4   You must support your argument with well-researched _____.
5   Critical thinking involves considering _____ ideas as well as concrete ones.
6   Paolo is looking for an artist to _____ a short story for him.
7   Mai _____ managed to work out the answer to her problem.
8   Can you _____ the word *discombobulate*?
9   The council has announced a new _____ to tackle the housing crisis.
10   The college has a good reputation and _____ it is in a great city.

Units 6–10

Complete the sentences using the words in the box.

> analysis   automatic   data   factor   relevant
> revise   specific   survey   techniques   vision

1   You should learn good study _____ so that you study efficiently.
2   According to a recent _____, the number of people who smoke has fallen by 20% in the last five years.
3   The information in your essay must be _____ to the topic.
4   The students are allowed one chance to _____ their test answers.
5   Poverty is an important _____ in the current immigration crisis.
6   Once you have collected the _____, email me your spreadsheet.
7   The information in my report was too general—not _____ enough to get a good mark.
8   In the final _____, it is not how much money you make, but how well you do your job that counts.
9   Drivers speeding on this highway face an _____ fine of $200.
10   Optometrists refer to normal eye sight as 20/20 _____.

Macmillan Education
4 Crinan Street
London N1 9XW
A division of Springer Nature Limited
Companies and representatives throughout the world

ISBN 978-1-380-00529-8

Designed by emc design ltd
Illustrated by emc design ltd and Carl Morris (Beehive Illustration) pp 123, 127, 149
Cover design by emc design ltd
Cover picture by Sam Parij (Eye Candy Illustration)/Getty Images/Moment Open/Alicia Llop
Picture research by Julie-anne Wilce

Authors' acknowledgements

Robyn Brinks Lockwood
I would like to thank Dorothy Zemach, the series editor, for asking me to be a part of the Skillful project, and the team at Macmillan for their editorial guidance. I also want to thank my family members who share my love for learning: my parents, Virgil and June, my brother and nephews, Tim, Darrin, and Nathan, and my husband, John.

The publishers would like to thank the following for their thoughtful insights and perceptive comments during the development of the material:

Dalal Al Hitty, University of Bahrain, Bahrain; Karin Heuert Galvão, i-Study Interactive Learning, São Paulo, Brazil; Ohanes Sakris, Australian College of Kuwait, Kuwait; Eoin Jordan, Xi'an Jiaotong-Liverpool University, Suzhou, China; Aaron Rotsinger, Xi'an Jiaotong-Liverpool University, Suzhou, China; Dr. Osman Z. Barnawi, Royal Commission Yanbu Colleges & Institutes, Yanbu, Saudi Arabia; Andrew Lasher, SUNY Korea, Incheon, South Korea; Fatoş Uğur Eskiçırak, Bahçeşehir University, Istanbul, Turkey; Dr. Asmaa Awad, University of Sharjah, Sharjah, United Arab Emirates; Amy Holtby, The Petroleum Institute, Abu Dhabi, United Arab Emirates; Dr. Christina Gitsaki, Zayed University, Dubai, United Arab Emirates.

The authors and publishers would like to thank the following for permission to reproduce their photographs:

Alamy/Roger Bamber p105(b), Alamy/Cultura Creative p60(tl), Alamy/Nick Gregory p136(br), Alamy/Myrleen Pearson p11(b), Alamy/Chris Rout p77(b), Alamy/Andrew Walters p51(c); **Getty Images**/Thomas Barwick p173(bl), Getty images/Howard Berman p47(c), Getty Images/Buena Vista Images pp80,81(t),(t), Getty Images/Color Blind Images p109(br), Getty Images/James Darell p101(b), Getty Images/Maksym Dragunov p157(cr), Getty Images/Robinson Ed p159(tr), Getty Images/EyeEm/Chongwen Li p88(cl), Getty Images/GgWink pp26,27(t),(t), Getty Images/Guntmar Fritz p158(bl), Getty Images/Mike Harrington p11(cr), Getty Images/Chris Hepburn p69(b), Getty Images/Hero Images p54(b), Getty Images/Hinterhaus Productions p145(br), Getty Images/kali9 p185(br), Getty images/macrovector p122(br), Getty Images/Tom Merton p88(cr), Getty Images/Morsa Images p88(l), Getty Images/Judd Patterson p157(cl), Getty Images/Pavliha p83(br), Getty Images/People Images p29(b), Getty Images/Philippe Sainte-Laudy Photography p122(bl), Getty images/David du Plessis p116,117(t),(t), Getty Images/Andrey Popov p173(br), Getty Images/Simon Ritzmann p88(r), Getty Images/KaPe Schmidt pp170,171(t),(t), Getty Images/Ariel Skelley p137(b), Getty Images/Stringer/ARIF ALI pp152,153(t),(t), Getty Images/Stringer/Boureima Hama pp8,9(t),(t), Getty Images Studio Box p98,99(t),(t), Getty Images/Nico Tondini p159(bl), Getty Images/Peter Unger pp72,73(b),(b), Getty Images/urbancow p37(br), Getty Images/View Pictures pp44,45(t),(t), Getty Images/Marilyn Angel Wynn pp134,135(t),(t), Getty Images/zhuda p155(b); **Macmillan Publishers Ltd**/Getty Images/Westend61 p122(bcl), Macmillan Publishers Ltd/PHOTODISC p166(bl); **Science Photo Library**/SMETEK pp32,33(bl),(b); **Shutterstock**/Katiekk p159(cr), Shutterstock/Nina Lishchuk p136(bc), Shutterstock/Maxx-Studio pp62,63(t),(t), Shutterstock/Photographee.eu p11(cl), Shutterstock/wavebreakmedia p122(bcr), Shutterstock/wowsty p136(bl); **Thomson Reuters** pp8(bl),2 6(bl),44(bl),62(bl),80(bl),98(bl),116(bl),134(bl),152(bl),170(bl), Thomson Reuters/Courtesy Wyss Institute at Harvard University, Courtesy Octo Telematics, Courtesy TV Globo.

Printed and bound in Poland by CGS
2023 2022 2021 2020 2019
17 16 15 14 13 12 11 10 9 8

PALGRAVE STUDY SKILLS

by bestselling author, **Stella Cottrell**

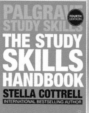

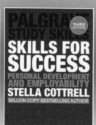

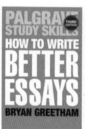
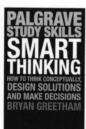
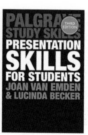

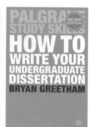

palgravestudyskills.com

f facebook.com/skills4study

🐦 twitter.com/skills4study